SAINTS AND SINNERS

SAINTS
AND
SINNERS

*Men and Ideas in the
Early Church*

by
KURT ALAND

translated by
WILHELM C. LINSS

FORTRESS PRESS
Philadelphia

This book is a translation of the third revised edition of *Kirchengeschichte in Lebensbildern dargestellt,* volume one, *Die Frühzeit* by Kurt Aland. Published by Wichern-Verlag, Berlin, 1962.

Library of Congress Catalog Card Number 76-123507

2353K69   Printed in U.S.A.   1-199

CONTENTS

JESUS—*Did He Really Live?*   1

LUKE—*Who Wrote the Gospels?*   4

PAUL—*The Gospel Goes to Europe*   8

STEPHEN—*First Apostle to the Gentiles*   11

BARNABAS—*An Unsung Missionary*   15

AQUILA AND PRISCILLA—*The Role of Women*   18

ONESIMUS—*The Problem of Wealth and Station*   23

JAMES, THE BROTHER OF THE LORD—*The End of Jewish Christianity*   29

PETER—*The Sinner's Comfort*   33

CLEMENT OF ROME—*What Was a Bishop?*   37

IGNATIUS OF ANTIOCH—*The Office of a Bishop*   40

POLYCARP OF SMYRNA—*Model Martyr*   45

SIMON THE MAGICIAN—*The Struggle with Gnosticism*   49

MARCION—*Apostle of the Strange God*   55

MONTANUS—*The Attempt to Reverse History*   62

THE APOLOGISTS—*Defenders of the Faith*   67

JUSTIN MARTYR—*Apologist and Martyr*   71

THE SCILLITAN MARTYRS—*History Written in Blood*   74

THE MARTYRS OF LYONS AND VIENNE—*They Prayed for Life*   78

IRENAEUS —*Guaranteeing the Faith*   82

CELSUS—*Serious Pagan Criticism*   87

CLEMENT OF ALEXANDRIA—*The Christian Scholar*   92

ORIGEN—*Controversial Theologian*   96

CALIXTUS OF ROME—*The Church Is for Sinners*   101

TERTULLIAN—*A Passionate Theologian*   106

CYPRIAN—*Outside the Church, No Salvation*   111

NOVATUS AND NOVATIAN—*Personal Ambition*   116

DIONYSIUS OF ALEXANDRIA—*How Is Jesus God?*   122

DIOCLETIAN—*Persecution Fails*   127

CONSTANTINE—*A Decisive Supporter*   133

DONATUS—*Defeat out of Victory*   138

ARIUS—*The Influence of a Dead Heretic*   144

ATHANASIUS—*Christ—Creature or Eternal Son?*   148

EUSEBIUS OF CAESAREA—*Father of Church History*   155

ANTHONY—*Hermit of the Desert*   160

PACHOMIUS—*Founder of Monasticism*   164

JULIAN THE APOSTATE—*Lapsed Christian—Last Pagan*   169

BASIL OF CAESAREA—*An Old Question Resolved*   174

DAMASUS OF ROME—*An Early Pope*   178

THEODOSIUS THE GREAT—*Not in a Vacuum*   185

AMBROSE OF MILAN—*An Impartial Bishop*   190

AUGUSTINE—*"Pick It Up, Read It"*   197

PELAGIUS—*The Adopted Heretic*   208

JOHN CHRYSOSTOM—*The Goldenmouthed Preacher*   214

NESTORIUS—*A New Controversy*   221

DIOSCURUS—*The Person of Christ*   230

LEO I—*The Papacy—A Finished Product*   238

JUSTINIAN—*A New Age Dawns*   244

JESUS

Did He Really Live?

A few decades ago a lively debate was carried on in many books and journals about whether there really had been such a person as Jesus. The debate was hot and heavy, and names like Kalthoff, Drews, and Jensen were on the lips of many. They and others maintained that Jesus was not a historical person at all but instead an ideal figure, a myth which embodied the religious and social longings of the masses. The debate soon subsided, and today only a few scholars are familiar with the names of these once-famous men whose books now collect dust. The fact is that even while all of this literature was being published (some of a sensational nature) scholars knew that such views were untenable. Even those who would have been happy had the views of Kalthoff, Drews, and others like them been confirmed gradually came to this conclusion.

It is quite surprising, therefore, to read in a history textbook used extensively in a certain section of Germany that the "Jesus myth" originated at a time of extraordinary social oppression, a time when people were taking refuge in religion and believed that a Messiah would deliver them. The book goes on to say: "The development of this myth was strongly influenced by Oriental myths. At first the myth was developed and transmitted orally. Later on it was committed to writing. In none of the historical works of that time do we find a word about the life of Jesus Christ." An informed person can only be astonished. These are exactly the same untenable, fantastic assertions which had been made years ago. And the author presents these views as if the earlier debate had never taken place!

It is remarkable that pseudoscientific criticism shows a preference for the earliest history of Christianity and applies to its study of that period arguments which are not used anywhere else. The textbook which contains the sentences just quoted speaks of Socrates, for example, as though the information we have about him were absolutely reliable. Socrates' outstanding role in the history of philosophy and the quest of the human spirit is uncontested, but how reliable is our knowledge concerning him? He himself did not write anything. And the textbook's claim that we do not find a word about Jesus in the historical works of his time can be applied to Socrates as well: everything we know about the great philosopher dates from a later period. Xenophon and Plato, our two principal sources of information on Socrates, vehemently contradict each other. Yet neither the author of the textbook mentioned nor anyone else seriously doubts that Socrates really lived, even though the historical evidence concerning him is by far inferior to that about the life of Jesus.

To be sure, the Gospels, which are the main sources of our knowledge about the life of Jesus, were not written until after his death, but they reach back into his lifetime, as we will see. Even without any of the Gospels, that Jesus lived would be a historical certainty. Just a few years after his death, Paul was converted to Christianity when he had a vision of Christ near Damascus. Although his letters contain very little specific information about Jesus' earthly life, they still give solid evidence that Jesus really lived. These letters testify to him directly and indirectly, from the first line to the last. All the letters of Paul were written before A.D. 64, at a time when many people who had seen Jesus with their own eyes were living. First Corinthians 15, for example, is evidence of the resurrection experience of the first disciples, equally convincing to any historian, Christian or not.

We could continue at length like this; but it is enough to say just a few words about the silence of the secular historians of the first century concerning the life of Jesus. Their silence is not so astonishing since Jesus lived in a very remote corner of the Roman Empire, an area in which no historian was interested. Nazareth, Bethlehem, Capernaum, Galilee—all these places lay completely beyond the interest of the historians of that time. Even the events in Jerusalem, which, by the way, took place in a very short span of time, could not have been regarded as significant in that period. First-century historians took scant notice even of other local, seemingly more important, events. Besides, there were only a few historians. Josephus was a Jew, and Jesus did not fall within the scope of his work. That leaves Suetonius and Tacitus, both of whom wrote after A.D. 100 and both of whom mention Christ and the Christians.

So the argument that none of the historical works of that time mentions the life of Jesus Christ is true only on the surface. Its strength as evidence is lost completely when we recall that at a very early date opponents of Christianity, Jews as well as Gentiles, circulated all kinds of slanders against Jesus, but at no time did they claim that the Jesus of the Christians never lived or that he was just a figment of their imagination. It remained for modern "scholars" to invent this argument, which is but one of the many attempts to escape the uncomfortable reality of Christ, who not only lived in the past but lives now and forever. The reality of his life proves itself in the life of his church which, despite all its weaknesses and shortcomings, despite all the sufferings and tribulation imposed by its opponents, has lived on for almost two thousand years. The reality of his life is verified by his enemies and the enemies of his church who, by their bitter hostility, unwittingly furnish proof that Christ was real not only in the first century but in all centuries. The reality of his life is verified anew in the hearts of the believers whom the Holy Spirit makes more certain than any historical evidence could ever do.

LUKE

Who Wrote the Gospels?

It is a great mistake for us to skip over the very first verses of the Gospel according to Luke as though they were of no importance. The fact is that they are of greatest significance for our evaluation not only of the Gospel of Luke but of all four Gospels.

This is what these verses say: "Inasmuch as many have undertaken to compile a narrative of the things which have been accomplished among us, just as they were delivered to us by those who from the beginning were eyewitnesses and ministers of the word, it seemed good to me also, having followed all things closely for some time past, to write an orderly account for you, most excellent Theophilus, that you may know the truth concerning the things of which you have been informed." This is what Luke writes to Theophilus, to whom he dedicates his book. It is apparent that Theophilus held an important position, and that he was probably a Christian; beyond that we know nothing about him. His name is mentioned in only one other place in Scripture, Acts 1:1. This is an example of how limited our knowledge about the earliest Christian churches is.

But we must be grateful for any information which is handed down to us. For when Luke and the other Evangelists wrote their accounts, and when Paul wrote to his congregations, none of them was thinking of posterity. They wrote for their day, and their sole desire was to serve their fellow Christians. Nevertheless, many

Christian writings and letters of the first century of our church have been preserved and handed down to us. This is a sign that what has come to us from the oldest Christian community is more reliable and trustworthy than has often been thought. Perhaps an example will demonstrate the point. How much has been preserved from the reign of Alexander the Great, who conquered a new world and who has been celebrated in history for his exploits and bravery? Alexander was deeply concerned that posterity should have a record of his deeds. Diaries were kept at court, and everything of importance was meticulously noted. Scholars and chroniclers accompanied him on all his expeditions; these men and other companions reported in detail the tremendous events of those days. Each of these chroniclers wrote with the intention of preserving an accurate account for posterity. But, of all this, practically nothing has come down to us except a few fragments and some quotes in the works of later writers.

Something else must be taken into consideration. Just as the Evangelists never thought that they were writing for posterity, so they never intended to write "history" in our sense, that is, to note every detail as in a diary. They presented the life of Jesus Christ, whose resurrection verified his words and deeds. From this point of view they collected the data preserved by the eyewitnesses, as Luke says in the opening words of his Gospel. Collections of sayings of the Lord as well as collections of his miraculous deeds probably came into existence at a very early date. But the immediate testimony, not the written report, stood in the foreground. As long as there were disciples in the community who were able to recount directly from their own experience (certainly these disciples numbered more than the twelve who made up the innermost circle of chosen followers around Jesus), written Gospels were not needed.

Only when the church extended beyond Jerusalem and Palestine, and death took the eyewitnesses one after the other, did disciples begin to gather the individual writings which up to this time had been scattered. Around the year A.D. 70 our Gospels were written. The oldest of them is the Gospel of Mark, which was used by

Luke and Matthew, both of whom had yet other sources at their disposal: a collection of Jesus' sayings and another collection that contained mostly parables. Even the Gospel of Mark had predecessors, and the Gospel of Luke was not the last to be written—the Gospel of John was written some twenty years later. Just as Luke says, there was an abundance of reports; gradually, they disappeared, and were replaced by the four Gospels as they are now found in our New Testament. Afterwards, in the second century and even later, still other reports about the life of Jesus were written. Certainly they contain some information which would substantially help to extend and complement our knowledge of the life and ministry of Jesus, for as said, our four Gospels never intended to report everything completely. Yet none of these is comparable to those that have been preserved, so their loss is not a great one. (It is significant that the so-called Gospel of Thomas, which since its discovery about fifteen years ago has received such widespread attention, has not brought to light any essentially new, genuine sayings of Jesus.) As important as it would be for us to possess details to supplement the reports of our four Gospels, let us mourn less for that which is lost than rejoice over that which has been preserved.

The attachment of the names of the Evangelists to the New Testament Gospels was a guarantee to earlier generations that the content of these Gospels was true. Today we have found it more profitable to look at the antecedent history of the Gospels which Luke explicitly mentions. When we do that we discover traces of the works of men whose names are unknown to us, the men who originally wrote the collections which were the source materials for the Gospels. We have also learned not to place too much emphasis on the names of Luke, Mark, Matthew, John in the titles of our Gospels: these names quite certainly were not in the original manuscripts but were added later. The old tradition, stemming from Papias, claimed that Peter's recollections were the basis of the Gospel of Mark, who was purported to have been Peter's aide and interpreter, although the Gospel itself does not mention any author's name. We should also note that according to tradition not the whole first Gospel, but only a collection of sayings of the Lord is attributed to Matthew, and that the Gospel according to Luke nowhere mentions Luke the physician, the travel companion of Paul, as its author. Likewise the Gospel according to John does not claim explicitly that it was written by the apostle John.

Therefore we should not claim more than the Gospels themselves claim, for what is important about the Gospels? Certainly not their authors! What is important is the Lord, the one of whom they tell. In his own good time he chose the writers of the Gospels, who, although their identity is unknown to us, are witnesses of his glory. And he who chose them now calls us to faith through them.

PAUL

The Gospel Goes to Europe

When Paul wrote his letter to the Romans, Christians were already living in the capital of the empire. These Christians were not numerous: they were neither influential nor prominent. However, by this time Christian congregations had existed in Europe for almost ten years—not in Italy but in Greece. The true cradle of European Christianity is Greece, even though the Roman congregation is assumed to be the oldest Christian congregation in Europe.

When and through whom did Christianity come to Greece and thus to Europe? Paul landed on Greek soil over nineteen hundred years ago, around A.D. 50. For nineteen hundred years now there have been men in Europe who in their worship and their prayers have called on Jesus Christ as their Lord. How much has happened since that time in European history! Great nations have come and gone. Empires that boasted they would last forever have fallen in ruins. Of some of these empires we can find hardly a trace. A host of wars have brought untold suffering and misery on mankind. Nevertheless, Christianity has spread over all of Europe, reaching out from those Greek congregations, overcoming and superseding all other, once powerful religions, until today its confessors, in numbers at least, have gained an absolute majority, unequaled in Europe by any other religious or ideological community. And all this despite oppression and frequent bloody persecution through the centuries down to our own time! If a proof were needed for the truth and genuineness of the Christian message, here it is. For this was not accomplished by men. The history of Europe shows us what men are able to accomplish! The extension of Christianity was possible not because of men but in spite of men, for in the history of Christianity we find repeated evidences of much human weakness, insufficiency, and error.

Paul did not plan to take Christianity to Europe. As reported in Acts 16, Paul was on his second missionary journey in Asia Minor to visit congregations he had founded on his first journey and to organize new ones. But the spirit of Jesus prevented him, and so instead he went to Troas, a seaport at the Western coast of Asia Minor. One night Paul had a vision: "A man of Macedonia was standing beseeching him and saying, 'Come over to Macedonia and help us' " (16:9). Along with his companions he concluded "that God had called us to preach the gospel to them" (16:10). Paul started out immediately, boarding a boat which took him to Neapolis, known today as Kavalla. We are familiar with the reports in Acts concerning Philippi, Thessalonica, Beroea, Athens, and Corinth, the places in Greece where he first ministered. Paul returned to Greece a second time, on his third missionary journey (Acts 20). On his third journey to Europe he came as a prisoner. Rome was the goal of this journey, and it was here that he died as a martyr and witness to his Lord Jesus Christ.

Paul travelled on foot through Palestine, Syria, Cyprus, Asia Minor, and Greece, but we do not know how active he was in Italy, and it is questionable whether he was ever in Crete or Spain, as some think. Only once is it reported that he rode (Acts 23:24), and at that time he was being taken as a prisoner from Jerusalem to Caesarea. His travelling was not that of a vacationing tourist with nothing else to do; he earned his keep by working with his own hands. His main work, however, was to evangelize, preach, teach, and because of this he was persecuted by Jews and Gentiles. He traversed this tremendous distance over a period of some fifteen years. When we trace his journeys on a map we marvel at the distance he covered. Those of his letters which have been preserved for us (1 Thessalonians is the oldest) were written within this short span of time, which is the only period of his life about which we possess any detailed information. We have only hints about his youth, the years prior to his ministry at Antioch (Acts 11), and the last years of his life. We must also marvel at the achievement of this man whose physical appearance was unimpressive and whose body was wracked by sickness! In a wonderful way God took hold of his life and directed his path from that day on the road to Damascus when the risen Lord appeared to him in splendor and glory, when Saul became Paul, and the fervid enemy and persecutor of Christianity became its greatest apostle! "For my power is made perfect in weakness" (2 Cor. 12:9)—not only then, nineteen hundred years ago, but even today and among us.

STEPHEN

First Apostle to the Gentiles

Paul's letter to the Roman congregation is our oldest testimony to the presence of Christians in Rome. Since other sources are lacking and even the Book of Acts is silent on the subject except for a few hints in chapter 28, we are completely dependent on this letter for information about the origin and form of the congregation in what was then the capital of the world. If Philippians was written in Rome, then the closing verses of that epistle also help us. On the basis of these two writings we can say several things, among them, that the congregation in Rome was not founded by Paul (Rom. 15:20–22). Rather, he wrote the letter to them in order to announce his intention to visit the Christians already in Rome. His previous sphere of influence had become too small for him, since he had fully preached the gospel "from Jerusalem and as far round as Illyricum" (Rom. 15:19). But Paul was not looking to Rome for its own sake. He wanted to visit Rome on the way to Spain (Rom. 15:24–29). From the Book of Acts we know that things turned out quite differently from the way Paul had thought, that his journey to Jerusalem led to imprisonment, and that he came to Rome as a prisoner and died there as a witness to his Lord. "Man proposes; God disposes."

The congregation at Rome consisted of Gentile Christians, so Paul was writing not to converted Jews but to converted Gentiles (see Rom. 1:5–6; 1:13; 11:13). There can be no doubt about this even though the letter also extensively treats questions which seem to apply particularly to readers of Jewish origin. We have before us here a type of early Christian congregation whose significance was not correctly recognized in earlier years—Gentile-Christian, yet founded independently of Paul and not shaped by his theology. At one time Paul's congregations were distinguished only from those which had had their origin in the missionary work of the Jerusalem congregation and from those which had consciously retained something of Judaism (we will speak in greater detail about these congregations in the section on James, the brother of the Lord). The church at Rome shows that the early history of Christianity is much more complex than had been assumed at first.

The Roman church was not the only one of its kind. There was, for instance, a congregation of exactly the same kind at Antioch, the capital of Syria, on the banks of the Orontes (which is not to be confused with Antioch in Pisidia, located in Asia Minor [Acts 13,14]). The church at Rome has had special significance for the history of Christianity because Rome was the capital of the empire, but the church at Antioch was probably much more important then. At Antioch Paul engaged in his first major activity (Acts 11:22–30), and from Antioch he started on his first missionary journey after being ordained by its congregation (Acts 13:1–3). According to Acts 11:26, "in Antioch the disciples were for the first time called Christians," a fact which puts the importance of this church into the proper light. Jerusalem, Antioch, the churches of Paul—this was the route by which Christianity spread throughout the world.

When the significance of the congregation at Antioch in the history of Christianity was recognized, one name, which until then had stood in the background, received a completely new reputation, and its bearer moved up in prominence to a place with the twelve apostles and Paul. The name is that of Stephen, through whose co-workers Antioch was evangelized. It was they who first preached the gospel no longer exclusively to Jews but also to Gentiles. Acts 10 tells us that Peter converted the Gentile centurion Cornelius, but this is quite obviously exceptional. It is significant that Peter at first struggled against preaching to Gentiles and needed a divine command, repeated three times. It is also significant that Peter had to defend himself and his baptism of Cornelius against the criticism of the other apostles and brethren (Acts 11). It was only the friends and followers of Stephen who consciously embarked upon a mission to the Gentiles: "Now those who were scattered because of the persecution that arose over Stephen traveled as far as Phoenicia and Cyprus and Antioch, speaking the word to none except Jews. But there were some of them, men of Cyprus and Cyrene, who on coming to Antioch spoke to the Greeks also, preaching the Lord Jesus. And the hand of the Lord was with them, and a great number that believed turned to the Lord" (Acts 11:19–21).

The names of these missionaries have not been handed down to us. They probably belonged to the circle of Stephen, who was their spiritual leader, as the report in Acts 6 proves beyond doubt. We do not know in detail the theological beliefs of this circle. We know only that the defense of Stephen is recorded in Acts 7. Even this speech, which, because of its defensive character, presents Stephen's theology only in excerpts, shows how critically Stephen stood up in opposing Judaism: "You stiff-necked people, uncircumcised in heart and ears, you always resist the Holy Spirit. As your fathers did, so do you. Which of the prophets did not your fathers persecute? And they killed those who announced beforehand the coming of the Righteous One, whom you have now betrayed and murdered, you who received the law as delivered by angels and did not keep it" (Acts 7:51–53).

The report in Acts 6 tells of the tensions which existed between the circle of Stephen and the rest of the early church at Jerusalem. The "Hellenists" (the Greek-speaking Christians at Jerusalem) felt offended by the strictly Jewish Christian part of the early church (the "Hebrews"). Even if this may have referred at first to external and superficial things, the opposition grew deeper. This is clearly shown by the fact that Stephen did not confine himself to the distribution of the gifts of love which had been entrusted to him by the apostles, but that he saw his true task to be that of preaching (Acts 6:7–8). And when persecution broke out after his death, his followers had to flee. The apostles, however, were able to remain in Jerusalem (Acts 8:1). They strictly maintained their Judaism along with the observance of the Jewish law. For this reason they and those who agreed with their way of thinking were unmolested by the authorities. The crack which had split the early church beneath the surface long before this now became openly visible. Christianity's turning from Jewish law and character was finally achieved through the work of Paul, and led to the founding of new congregations which stretched from Antioch to Rome and into all the world.

BARNABAS

An Unsung Missionary

When we think of the spreading of Christianity in the early period we usually think of Paul. We have the idea that within a single quarter of a century this man single-handedly carried Christianity, hitherto closely confined to Jerusalem, to the far corners of the earth. Paul was indeed responsible for much of this extension. But—and this has to be emphasized—he was neither the first nor the only missionary to carry the gospel to the Gentile world. Nor were Stephen's followers the only ones besides Paul who were active in missionary work. It must be borne in mind that there were a large number of people, whose identities are unknown to us for the most part, who had dedicated their lives to the spreading of Christianity.

Only a few of them emerge so clearly in the New Testament that we can speak with any degree of certainty about their personality or the influence and significance of their work. One might think of Philip, who worked in Samaria as a missionary and who, on a journey, converted the "Ethiopian," the minister of Candace, the Queen of the Ethiopians (Acts 8:26–39). But Philip evidently belonged to Stephen's circle; Acts 6 names him as one of the seven deacons. For this reason we do not devote a separate section to him in this book.

Actually, there is only one other pre-Pauline missionary about whom we really know something—Barnabas. We know relatively little about his life, but even that little suggests the great importance of the man. Soon after the founding of the church, this Jewish priest from Cyprus became a believer and put all his possessions at the disposal of his congregation, in which he undoubtedly held a highly respected position. When news came to Jerusalem that a new congregation had been founded at Antioch, the apostles sent him there for a visitation. This was a highly responsible task, one usually carried out only by the apostles themselves.

Barnabas' behavior shows that he knew he held a degree of authority. It was he who first received Paul, and probably it was he who first recognized Paul's potential and led him to Antioch. Previously, when Paul had come from Damascus to Jerusalem (Acts 9:27), it had been Barnabas who smoothed the way for Paul to approach the apostles and the congregation, for at first they had doubted the genuineness of his conversion. Now, in Antioch, it was he who opened for Paul the first major field of work. The visible sign of their cooperation, which was decisive for the beginning of Christianity's spread into the pagan world, is the fact that the two of them together were singled out by the congregation for the missionary journey. This teamwork dissolved later, when Paul undertook his second missionary journey alone. The events until then were such that Barnabas was assured of a central position in the history of early Christianity. But after his separation from Paul he faded from the scene.

Through Barnabas we gain insight into the otherwise closed world of those missionaries to the Gentiles before Paul of whom the New Testament speaks only occasionally and incidentally. Silas (also called Silvanus), Demas, Epaphras, and especially Timothy and Titus no doubt were not only Paul's aides but also independent missionaries and founders of congregations, important figures not only in the history of missions but in all of church history because of their role as missionaries. Second Corinthians shows indirectly what influence these missionaries could exert. Paul was having some difficulties with the congregation at Corinth. Neither by his letters nor by his personal presence was he able to overcome a split which divided the congregation and assert himself against his opponents there. But what neither he nor Timothy was able to do was achieved by the presence of Titus at Corinth. Second Corinthians is the testimony of joy over the fact that peace has returned to the congregation and that the old relationship with Paul has been restored.

The New Testament tells very little about others who helped carry the message of the gospel to the Gentile world. It is not a historical book in the modern sense of history: it is concerned not with the glory of men but with the glory of Him to whom these men dedicated their lives.

AQUILA AND PRISCILLA

The Role of Women

We have already noted that other missionaries besides Paul were active in taking Christianity to the Gentile world. Their number must have been larger than the letters of the New Testament and the Book of Acts would suggest, even though none of them, including Timothy and Titus, approached the prominence of Paul. There were also missionaries who worked independently, without relationship to the congregation of Antioch or to Paul. We read about some of them in Acts 18 and 19.

One of these missionaries was Apollos, a Jew from Alexandria who had taken up residence in Ephesus. The Book of Acts says of him that he was "fervent in [the] spirit [of the Lord]" and "well versed in the scriptures," and that he preached the gospel of Jesus Christ "accurately" (Acts 18:24–25). We do not know where or how he became a Christian. One ancient writer claims that Apollos had been instructed in Christianity in his native land. If that is correct, we would have here the oldest evidence for the existence of the Christian church in Egypt. Actually, only one thing is definite: he must have followed a completely different line of development from that of the Christians evangelized by Paul. Apollos knew only the baptism of John to repentance, not baptism in the name of Jesus Christ.

Apollos covered a wide territory; he worked at Ephesus and went from there to Greece where, according to Acts 18:27–28, he was a great help to the Christians, largely because he had an effective manner of interpreting the Scriptures to the Jews. From Paul's report in his first letter to the Corinthians we get the impression that Apollos had considerable success in Corinth (see 1 Cor. 3:4–6; 4:6). Titus 3:13 indicates that Apollos also stayed in Crete, but nothing more is said about him. This does not imply that there was nothing else worth reporting, but, as has been stressed in earlier chapters, the New Testament just is not a history book bent upon recording all the details of early Christian history.

It was apparently in Ephesus that Apollos met for the first time leading representatives of Paul's school of Christianity. These representatives were a man and woman, Aquila and Priscilla—or more exactly, Priscilla and Aquila, for Acts 18:26 puts the woman in the first place. They received Apollos and "expounded to him the way of God more accurately"; that is, they enlarged and deepened his previous knowledge of Christianity. Aquila and Priscilla (or Prisca, the form of the name used in the letters of Paul), had come from Rome a few years earlier. Because of an edict of the emperor Claudius (A.D. 41–54) which banned Jews from the capital, they had left Italy and settled in Corinth. (A number of such anti-Jewish edicts had been issued by Roman emperors.) At Corinth they had resumed their trade of tent-making. When Paul came to Corinth he worked in their shop in order to earn his own living. It was not his custom to be dependent upon his congregations for his support. Aquila and Priscilla finally left Corinth with Paul and moved to Ephesus (Acts 18:19; 1 Cor. 16:19), where they probably remained until the death of Claudius. Soon after, they returned to Rome—upon the death of the emperor his edict against the Jews had become invalid. The Epistle to the Romans (16:3) mentions them as being among the Roman Christians to whom Paul sent personal greetings. In fact, their names stand at the head of the list: "Greet Prisca and Aquila, my fellow workers in Christ Jesus, who risked their necks for my life, to whom not only I but also all the churches of the Gentiles give thanks." In this way Paul publicly rendered his thanks to this couple. We do not know on what occasion they risked their lives for Paul; perhaps it was in connection with the events in Ephesus to which Paul refers in 2 Corinthians 1:8 and in 1 Corinthians 15:32. Evidently, then, this couple extended its activity and influence far beyond the confines of a single congregation.

It is quite significant that in the Romans passage Priscilla is again mentioned first. This is not just a form of courtesy. Priscilla is also mentioned first in Acts 18:18, 26 and 2 Timothy 4:19. Aquila is mentioned first only in 1 Corinthians 16:19 and Acts 18:2. The great historian Adolf von Harnack was not the first to suspect that of this couple the woman played the leading role. Many centuries ago one of the church fathers, Chrysostom, assumed that it was Priscilla who gave Apollos, the highly educated Alexandrian, his instruction in the Christian faith. Harnack went so far as to suggest that Priscilla may have been the author of the Epistle to the Hebrews. Whether that is correct is a matter yet to be decided. One thing is certain: Priscilla was a woman highly esteemed in the Christian congregations, one who occupied an important position.

In our day it is often thought that women played only a subordinate role in the early church and that what they did was of no great significance. To be sure, there were no women in the Lord's immediate circle of disciples. Only men belonged to the inner circle of disciples (in the most narrow sense of the word; for besides the Twelve there was, for example, the circle of the Seventy [see Luke 10:1, 17]). But it is certainly not correct to interpret this, as is often done today, as an argument against bestowing the full pastoral office on women.

Quite obviously women were among the constant followers of the Lord and belonged to his closest circle of confidants (see Luke 8:1-2; Mark 15:40-41). The narratives of Mary and Martha are so well known that we only have to mention their names, but we often overlook the fact that women stood under the cross (Mark 15:40-41; Matt. 27:55; Luke 23:49, 55; John 19:25), that women stayed at the tomb when the disciples had fled, and that according to the Gospels the risen Lord appeared first to women. Mark 16:9–11 is a summary of the other reports: "Now when he rose early on the first day of the week, he appeared first to Mary Magdalene . . . . She went and told those who had been with him, as they mourned and wept. But when they heard that he was alive and had been seen by her, they would not believe it." The Jerusalem congregation gathered in the house of Mary, the mother of Mark (Acts 12:12). The first Christian church we know of on European soil came into being in the house of Lydia, the seller of purple goods (Acts 16:14–15).

Again and again the Book of Acts points to the important role women played in the extension of Christianity (for example, 17:4, 12). Women also played a role in the public worship. The four prophesying daughters of Philip (Acts 21:9) were not a spiritual oracle that officiated only at home. Their prophesying is to be explained in light of 1 Corinthians 11:5, where women pray or prophesy in the service; that is, they have a share in the pastoral office. In the same letter, however, there is the much-discussed saying: "As in all the churches of the saints, the women should keep silence in the churches [that is, in the meetings of the congregation]. For they are not permitted to speak, but should be subordinate, as even the law says. If there is anything they desire to know, let them ask their husbands at home. For it is shameful for a woman to speak in church" (1 Cor. 14:34–36). Here Jewish custom asserts itself, as is indicated by the reference to the Jewish law. This passage is only a demand of Paul, not a description of what actually went on in the Corinthian church, something about which we learn in 1 Corinthians 11:5. (By the way, it is rather striking that a number of manuscripts put the verses strikingly behind 14:40, which in general would suggest that the text here is not in order.)

The demand of 1 Corinthians 14:34–35 soon became the norm for all the Christian church. First Timothy 2:12 states briefly and succinctly: "I permit no woman to teach or to have authority over men; she is to keep silent." Indeed, women still had a great influence in the Christian church of the second century, but it was precisely their influence which caused them to lose their former high position. They played a leading part in the heretical movements known as Montanism and Gnosticism. From then on the church would no longer grant women offices of even minor significance. Thereafter the church invested women only with "serving" functions (Rom. 16:1 mentions the "deaconess" Phoebe).

Today things are changing, and probably rightly so. One may have varying opinions about the special place or character of a pastoral office extended to women, but women can no longer be arbitrarily excluded. Even Paul—the same Paul who wrote 1 Corinthians 14:34-35—declared in Galatians 3:28: "There is neither Jew nor Greek, there is neither slave nor free, there is neither male nor female; for you are all one in Christ Jesus." Christianity has given women equal rights—the equality which does not deny their uniqueness, but at the same time closes no area of life to them. One cannot, then, exclude them from preaching the word and from the pastoral office.

ONESIMUS

The Problem of Wealth and Station

All the letters of the apostle Paul which we possess are genuinely letters; that is, they are writings addressed to very definite recipients in very definite situations with very definite needs. Obviously each letter contains matters of general validity which could have been of importance to other congregations also, but each was completely intelligible and understandable only to the recipients to whom it was originally addressed. This accounts for the manifold difficulties which the general reader and even the scholar encounter when they try to understand every detail of Paul's letters. The most personal of Paul's letters is the letter to Philemon, which Paul wrote toward the end of his life.

Philemon was evidently a well-to-do Christian of Asia Minor, probably in Colossae. One of his slaves, Onesimus, had escaped. It was after his escape that Onesimus met Paul, probably in Rome, where this letter most likely originated. There Onesimus was converted to Christianity by the imprisoned missionary. A completely new situation was created for the escapee by this experience. The heathen slave Onesimus could escape his master, but could the Christian Onesimus remain an escapee? We do not know what discussions took place between Paul and him concerning this question. Nor do we know whether Onesimus voluntarily decided to return or whether he needed the persuasion, perhaps even the urgent persuasion, of Paul and his companions. In any case,

Onesimus did return to his master. The Epistle to Philemon is the letter that Paul sent along with him. Paul wanted to retain Onesimus as his personal aide (v. 13), but he did not want to make a change in the situation without knowing Philemon's views. So he sent Onesimus back in order that Philemon would have him forever, "no longer as a slave but more than a slave, as a beloved brother" (v. 16).

During the last century this letter has been declared spurious a number of times. The charge has been made that this is not a genuine letter of Paul but rather a tendentious forgery aimed at resolving the matter of slavery. Nothing could be farther from the truth. The letter to Philemon bears the clear imprint of Paul's striking personality. Who but he could have written such a convincing, human, and spiritually outstanding letter? Furthermore, the letter does not by any means propose a solution to the problem of slavery. Only Onesimus, as an individual, is in view: nothing at all is said about slavery as such or about the Christian's attitude toward it. The letter does not even completely clarify what is to be done with Onesimus. Paul offers to reimburse Philemon personally for all the loss he may have suffered as a result of the slave's escape, but at the same time he intimates that he would not expect Philemon to press a claim for reimbursement of damages. He says that he relies on Philemon to do even more than Paul asks of him. Does this suggest the indirect request for the emancipation of Onesimus? Perhaps, perhaps not; we cannot say with certainty.

Only this much is sure: Paul demands of Philemon a new attitude toward Onesimus. Paul's word to the Galatians (3:28) is valid here too: among Christians "there is neither slave nor free." Position and origin count for nothing: Christians are a new creation and are of equal position and equal origin. They are one in Christ, and in light of this truth all prior differences are eliminated. Christianity works a revolution, but this revolution works from the inside to the outside. It does not change the external conditions of life in order to change men, but it changes men, and through that change creates a change in external circumstances.

In a Christian household the master is still master and the slave is still slave, seen from the outside, but in truth they are brothers with equal rights and equal duties. And where they are not brothers, their Christianity is counterfeit.

This is the way everything the New Testament says about social problems is to be understood. Slaves are mentioned in several places. In the era of the New Testament they were an integral part of the economic order. It was inconceivable that a society without slaves could exist. Nowhere in the New Testament is there a demand for the abolition of slavery. For Christians abolition would have bordered on Utopia, for generally only slaves were Christians, whereas their masters were adherents of the old religions and philosophies. Even when the masters were converts to Christianity, they were not commanded to release their slaves. Everyone, according to Paul, was to remain as he was when he was called (see 1 Cor. 7:20): this is the common denominator to which the attitude of the New Testament can be reduced. "For he who was called in the Lord as a slave [that is, he who was a slave when he became a Christian], is a freedman of the Lord. Likewise he who was free when called [that is, when he became a Christian], is a slave of Christ" (1 Cor. 7:22). Of course, it happened often that a slave owner who became a Christian released his slaves. It is also true that in later years the church bought freedom for slaves by purchasing them from their masters (usually heathens). But never was there a recognition of an inherent right of Christian slaves to be made freedmen.

Was Christianity, then, a religion which condoned the vested interests of established society? Indeed not! Rather the opposite was true. Granted, from the beginning there were well-to-do people among the Christians, as the Book of Acts indicates in several places. For example, in Acts 13:12 it is implied that the proconsul Sergius Paulus became a Christian. Acts 17:4 says that "not a few of the leading women" in Thessalonica were converted. Something similar is reported in Acts 17:12 about Beroea. But on the whole such people were a small minority among the early

Christians. In 1 Corinthians 1:26–29 Paul speaks of the makeup of the Corinthian congregation: "For consider your call, brethren; [when you became Christians] not many of you were wise according to worldly standards [literally: according to the flesh], not many were powerful, not many were of noble birth; but God chose what is foolish in the world to shame the wise, God chose what is weak in the world to shame the strong, God chose what is low and despised in the world, even things that are not, to bring to nothing things that are, so that no human being might boast in the presence of God." What Paul writes here about the church in the city of Corinth no doubt holds true also of the other congregations which he founded and of early Christian congregations in general. Again and again we find this observation confirmed by non-Christians as well. The noble and educated non-Christians of the first centuries looked with contempt on the Christian, for to them the Christian belonged to the dregs of humanity, and any member of the noble class who became a Christian had to realize that at the moment of commitment he would be an outcast from his social class in every way.

Not a few passages in the Gospels are directed emphatically against earthly riches. Just glance through the Gospel of Luke: "Woe to you that are rich," says the Lucan version of the Sermon on the Mount (6:24). The apostles are sent out without possessions: "Take nothing for your journey, no staff, nor bag, nor bread, nor money; and do not have two tunics" (9:3; compare 10:4). To the parable of the rich fool (12:13–21) is attached the warning against earthly worries (12:22–34): "Sell your possessions, and give [them away as] alms" (12:33). The rich man goes to Hades; the beggar Lazarus into paradise (16:19–31). Luke 18:25 says "it is easier for a camel to go through the eye of a needle than for a rich man to enter the kingdom of God." These are just a few examples, but all of them speak a clear language.

Still, from a sociological standpoint, early Christianity was a highly diversified body of people, and the church soon felt the tensions which resulted from the varied social backgrounds of its members. Paul had to reprimand the Corinthians for disorder (due in part to the cleavage in the congregation between the haves and the have-nots), at the common meals of the congregation (1 Cor. 11:20–22). And the epistle of James (2:1–13) speaks sharply against those Christians who measure the position of a member of the congregation according to his possessions. Nevertheless, except for scattered instances, there was no social problem in Christianity during the first three centuries. It was not unusual for a slave to become bishop of a large congregation such as that of Rome, which no doubt counted among its members quite a few noble and rich people. It was considered self-evident that the Christians would take care of widows and orphans as well as of all poor and sick persons. As late as the fourth century the simplicity and poverty of monasticism were held up as an ideal, and this was not a narcotic proffered to comfort the poor in their misery or an excuse to mollify them.

Monasticism, however, was a warning signal, for it had something of a protest character. As early as the third century, and then finally when Christianity achieved equal rights under Constantine and was on the way to absolute supremacy under his sons, the church came increasingly into contact with the world, and something of the world's spirit rubbed off on it. If at first the bishops almost without exception came from the lower strata of society, by the third century we find bishops coming from the privileged classes. By the fourth century bishops were chosen from among the first families of the empire.

Prior to Constantine the congregations had such modest worldly goods as congregational treasuries, church buildings, cemeteries, but they possessed them as if they did not possess them. Each persecution endangered not only the possessions of each individual Christian but also those of the congregations. This did not change until the reign of Constantine and his sons. Then the churches through the donations of the emperors and in other ways not infrequently became large landowners and their bishops became noble lords who in their prominence and dress ranked with high

27

officials. This change deeply affected the internal structure of the congregations and of Christianity itself, until finally the gospel's exhortation about worldly goods was forgotten and the church became far removed from its origins. All the protests of monasticism, the new waves of protest which arose during the Middle Ages, and even the protest which was voiced by members of the hierarchy were in vain. Only the Reformation would be able to bring about a basic change.

JAMES, THE BROTHER OF THE LORD

The End of Jewish Christianity

In his *Church History,* Eusebius offers several quotations from a writing, otherwise lost, of Hegesippus, a Christian author of the last half of the second century. In one of these quotations we find a description of the apostle James: "The charge of the church passed to James the brother of the Lord, together with the Apostles. He was called the 'Just One' by all men from the Lord's time to ours, since many are called James, but he was holy from his mother's womb. He drank no wine or strong drink, nor did he eat flesh; no razor went upon his head, he did not anoint himself with oil, and he did not go to the baths. He alone was allowed to enter into the sanctuary, for he did not wear wool but linen, and he used to enter the temple alone and be found kneeling and praying for forgiveness for the people. So from his excessive righteousness he was called the Just One and *Oblias,* that is in Greek, 'Rampart of the people and of righteousness,' as the prophets declare concerning him."

This description offers a valuable supplement and confirmation of what we know from the New Testament about the Lord's brother James. Right after the Ascension, before Pentecost, we find James among the apostles (Acts 1:13–14). After the death of Jesus he assumed the leadership of the church in Jerusalem and became its spiritual head. Whereas Peter was often absent from Jerusalem, evangelizing and supervising the outlying congregations, James evidently did not leave the city.

His name characterizes a particular kind of Christianity. He not only held fast to the Jewish law and the faith of his fathers in every detail, but he also had a circle of like-minded persons around him who advocated that this attitude be followed everywhere. What Paul reports in his letter to the Galatians (2:11–13) is significant. He relates that in Antioch, Peter, in line with the attitude of that local church and also with the views of Paul, assumed a freer attitude toward the Jewish law. But when followers of James came to Antioch, he and others with him, for fear of James, gave up table fellowship with the Gentile Christians.

James was, then, the embodiment of strict Jewish Christianity, and the earliest church in Jerusalem was a reflection of him. Here the Sabbath was strictly observed; Jewish dietary laws and the laws of fasting prevailed, even though the congregation probably knew that Jesus himself had not kept them, as the Gospels report again and again (for example, Mark 2:18–23; 2:23–28; 3:1–6; 7:1–8). The center of this Jewish Christianity was the temple, where followers of Jesus found themselves associated with the other Jews. Jesus was the Messiah—that was the knowledge which they possessed beyond Judaism, which was still waiting for the Messiah to come. But otherwise these Jewish Christians did not believe that the law should be abolished, nor did they consider themselves adherents to a religion apart from Judaism. On the contrary, they were very careful to hold fast to every consciousness of oneness with those Jews who had not yet come to faith in Christ. They hoped to lead their Jewish brethren gradually to the acknowledgement that the Messiah had come.

Today we take it quite for granted that James was a Christian who was convinced of the fact that, in Jesus, the Savior, the Son of God, had come to earth. But that was not so obvious. For, as certain as it is that James, after the resurrection of Jesus, was a believing Christian, it is also clear that during the lifetime of Jesus he was both negative toward him and his message and completely without understanding for his brother. The same is true of Jesus' whole family. We read in Mark 3:21 that when his relatives heard of his preaching and teaching activity, they went out to seize him, "for they said, 'He is beside himself.'" The alienation of Jesus from his family, as it is reported in Mark 3:31–35, Matt. 12:46–50, and Luke 8:19–22, is understood correctly only when the attitude of his family is considered. If one's own family persists in unbelief, the tie is cut off for the sake of the fellowship with the believers. Ties of faith are stronger than ties of blood.

Thus there was a deep break in the life of James. We do not know when this change from unbelief to belief took place. If we did not possess 1 Corinthians it would remain a complete puzzle to us. But we know from the report of the resurrection in 1 Corinthians 15:7 that Jesus appeared to his brother James as well as to others. This oldest report which we have of the resurrection is often neglected today in favor of the reports of the Gospels. Having seen the Risen One, James must have been overwhelmingly convinced that the Crucified One was the Son of God after all. That which all the words and miraculous deeds of Jesus during his lifetime could not achieve with James was achieved by the appearance of the risen Christ; James was brought from unbelief to faith. With him his other brothers were so overwhelmed that they, too, joined the circle of the disciples and accepted with James the fate which was prepared for the Christians by a hostile world.

For despite his strict observance of all Jewish ceremonies and his zealous keeping of the very letter of the Jewish law, James was not spared the death of a martyr. Eusebius' quotation of Hegesippus relates in detail the circumstances surrounding the death of James. The Pharisees and scribes were horrified by the increasing number of fellow Jews converting to Christianity, and asked James to intervene. Misjudging his real attitude, they hoped, with his help, to be able to contain the spread of Christianity. At Easter they arranged for James to warn the people against Jesus and his teaching from the pinnacle of the temple. Instead, he testified to Jesus as the Messiah, the Christ. The enraged Pharisees and scribes pushed James from the pinnacle. When he survived the fall, they stoned him. When one of the priests interceded for James, one of the group, a fuller by trade, struck James on the head with his fuller's tool and brought about his death. Even if this account does contain some embellishment, the testimony of the Jewish historian Josephus in his *Antiquities* confirms that James died as a martyr for his faith in the year 61 or 62 (even before Peter and Paul), painfully executed by the Jews.

The early church in Jerusalem did not want to be separated from the Jewish people, it was the Jewish people who rejected the church. Because of the death of James—and probably other similar events—the early church left Jerusalem and, according to Eusebius, was directed by a revelation to go to Pella, a city east of the Jordan River. Pella was a pagan city, despised and condemned by the Jews. Shortly afterward the Jewish war of liberation erupted, and Jews waged bloody battles with the Roman troops over a period of several years. Finally, in the summer of A.D. 70, Jerusalem was conquered and destroyed. With Jerusalem's destruction the temple, the true center of Judaism, fell into oblivion along with its whole religious organization. This event was looked upon by Christians throughout the world, then and later, as God's punishment upon Jewry for the crucifixion of Jesus. The Jewish cult of sacrifice came to an end with the destruction of the temple. The abolition of the law, the basis of Jewish Christianity, lay revealed to the eyes of all.

Jewish Christianity lost its influence over the mushrooming growth of the Christian church when it moved from Jerusalem. It dropped from sight although it continued to lead a modest existence for several centuries, during which time it was influenced and changed by many foreign ideas. The gospel, however, continued on its way, and a new world began to take shape.

PETER

The Sinner's Comfort

Time and again the name of Peter turns up in the Gospels. Several chapters of the Book of Acts are devoted to the description of his activity. Paul mentions him several times in his letters. There are two letters under his name in our New Testament. Yet all of this material is not sufficient for us to be able to present a complete biography of Peter. We only have bits and pieces of information to work with.

Peter's home was at Capernaum in Galilee, a town on the shore of the Sea of Tiberias. He, along with his brother Andrew, earned his living as a fisherman. There can be no doubt that Peter was married, a matter which is significant because of the requirement of the Roman Catholic church that its clergy be unmarried. In fact, the healing of Peter's mother-in-law was one of the first of Jesus' miraculous deeds. According to Mark's Gospel, Peter and Andrew were the first disciples called by the Lord. Very early we see Peter distinguished in many ways from the other disciples. For example, when the Twelve are enumerated in the Gospels, Peter is mentioned first. Then, too, Peter and the sons of Zebedee, James and John, and occasionally Peter's brother Andrew, are noted among the disciples as the circle of Jesus' special intimates. He was the spokesman for the disciples at the confession of Caesarea Philippi. Furthermore, he is distinguished by the honorable surnames Peter and Cephas, which mean "the rock." This name was given to him by Jesus following the confession at Caesarea Philippi: "You are Peter, and on this rock I will build my church, and the powers of death shall not prevail against it. I will give you the keys of the kingdom of heaven, and whatever you bind on earth shall be bound in heaven, and whatever you loose on earth shall be loosed in heaven" (Matt. 16:18–19).

Bitter controversy has raged over these words of Jesus. Protestants have denied their genuineness, but probably wrongly. In any case, according to the manuscript tradition of the Greek New Testament, there is no reason to assume that Matthew 16:18–19 was not originally in the Gospel. However, it is quite a different question whether the Roman Catholic church is justified in basing its claim to be the one true church on these words of the Lord. After all, these words were spoken to Peter. What makes them apply to the Roman church as well? It is likely that Peter went to Rome and that he died there, although there is no absolute proof of this. It is not likely that the real grave of the real Peter actually lies under the Church of Saint Peter in Rome. There is just no way of proving such a thing. Yet a short stay of Peter in Rome and his death there as a martyr can be assumed as very highly probable.

Furthermore, it is out of the question to think of Peter as the first bishop of the Roman church in the sense of the later papacy. What is said in Matthew 16:18–19 is said to Peter alone. It says that *Peter* is to be the rock on which the Lord will build the church, not a line of successors who were "bishops of Rome." Such bishops, as we shall see in later chapters, were not successors of Peter in the full sense of that word. And if the authority to bind and loose, that is, the authority to forgive sins, was given to Peter then we must point to Matthew 18:18 where the same authority is conferred on all apostles and, as the context here makes clear, on all clergymen, in fact on the whole church.

Aside from making him prominent and distinguished, there are many other aspects of Peter the Gospel reveals. In the same chapter

(Matthew 16) which tells us of the praise Jesus bestowed on Peter, we find that the Lord also said: "Get behind me, Satan! You are a hindrance to me; for you are not on the side of God, but of men" (16:23)—that is a fierce rejection. "Rock of the church" and "Satan" both in a single chapter! It was Peter who wanted to walk over water to the Lord, but he failed the test (Matt. 14:24–31). It was Peter who, before the arrest of Jesus, protested: "If I must die with you, I will not deny you" (Mark 14:31). But just as earnestly he denied the Lord after the arrest: "He began to invoke a curse on himself and to swear, 'I do not know this man'" (Mark 14:71).

Finally, it is again Peter whom we meet at Antioch playing a double role (Gal. 2). After first living with the Gentile Christians as one of them, he held himself aloof from them when the representatives of the Jerusalem congregation, who advocated a strict Jewish Christianity, arrived. This was not the first controversy in the history of the Christian church. Much earlier there had been disputes about the observance of the Jewish law by Gentile Christians (Acts 15). The issue was never resolved but a compromise had been agreed to. Now, however, Peter's conduct at Antioch opened the entire question once more. Peter's action not only could not be justified, but also caused a great disturbance in the Antioch congregation. We do not know the results of the encounter between Paul and Peter. Paul vehemently opposed him before the assembled congregation, and we then hear nothing more in Acts about the life and activity of Peter after the apostolic council. After Acts 15, which tells of the apostolic council, the Book of Acts is silent about him. Some think that he worked as a counter-apostle to Paul, following him on his journeys, and attempting to lead Gentile Christians over to Jewish Christianity. This is only an assumption, but the faction in the Corinthian congregation which adhered to Peter (1 Cor. 1:12), and Paul's remarks in the letter to the Galatians make one somewhat suspicious. What Peter did after the apostolic council mentioned in Acts 15 and how he met his end are matters shrouded in darkness.

Peter's life was a genuinely human combination of bright light
and deep shadow. It was Luther who pointed repeatedly to the
shadows in the life of Peter, just as he said often enough (as para-
doxical as this may sound), that he rejoiced that even Judas
Iscariot was counted among the disciples. The dark side of Peter's
life gives great comfort to the heart weighed down under sin and
despair—the comforting certainty of the grace of God. God, who
permitted sinners to be among the closest followers of his Son,
will show himself gracious to us too, even though our weakness,
our doubt, and our despair, which are the work of Satan in us,
constantly try to convince us of the contrary.

CLEMENT OF ROME

What Was a Bishop?

When did the apostles die? James, the son of Zebedee, died some-time during the reign of Herod Agrippa I (41–44); his brother John probably died around the same time. James, the brother of the Lord, was martyred in the year 61 or 62. Peter and Paul are assumed to have been put to death during the persecution of the Christians by Nero in the year 64. None of these died a natural death; they all fell victim to persecution as martyrs for their Lord Jesus Christ.

By A.D. 70 only a few of the original disciples of the Lord would have been alive. In time those who had not died a martyr's death died of natural causes. Only those who had met the Lord when they were very young might still have been alive then. Thus a new day dawned, a time when the church no longer counted among its members brethren who could tell first hand of the deeds and words of the Lord. This was the time when individual Gospel narratives, which had hitherto existed separately, were combined into whole books, as Luke describes in the first verses of his Gospel.

We call this period the postapostolic era. From it we have inherited many writings through which we learn a great deal about Christianity after the demise of the apostles. We possess letters similar to those of the New Testament, regulations known as church orders, a sermon, an exhortatory writing, and a book similar to Revelation. For a long time these writings enjoyed a status similar to that held today by our New Testament.

Even in our day the Apostolic Fathers, those who led the church after the death of the apostles, are held in high esteem. Next to the New Testament the writings of these men are the oldest documents of the Christian church, and they have exercised a great influence on its development. Even though they are practically unknown to most Christians today, they still contain many sections which can stand on a level with the New Testament and which express the timeless and basic truths of the Christian faith.

In this chapter we want to consider the oldest of these writings, *1 Clement*. It is designated "first" because there is a second letter of Clement which is not really a letter but a sermon, in fact, the oldest preserved Christian sermon outside of the New Testament. It was not, however, written by the author of the first letter. *First Clement* was written in Rome and addressed to the congregation at Corinth, where disunity and conflict had broken out. The letter admonishes the errant congregation to restore harmony.

The question which concerns us here is, who was the author of the letter? The ancient church thought that it was that Clement, of whom Paul speaks in the letter to the Philippians (4:3). Several legends have been attached to his name. A consul, Titus Flavius Clement, a member of the imperial household and a Christian, was martyred in the persecution under Emperor Domitian. It was widely assumed that he was the author. This is certainly not correct despite the name and despite the fact that *1 Clement* was written during the reign of Emperor Domitian, around the year 95 when that ruler began to persecute Christians first in Rome and then throughout the empire. The Revelation of John in the New Testament is a document of the general persecution, *1 Clement* a document of the persecution in the city of Rome. Although persecution of the church in Rome had been going on for some time and was increasing, Clement was able to give detailed attention to the needs of another congregation.

Quite certainly the author did not write in the capacity of a private individual. The letter is written in the name of and on behalf of the whole Roman congregation. Clement wrote as its commissioned officer and trustee, as its bishop. The Catholic church, therefore, lists him as one of the popes. As far back as the second century Irenaeus mentioned Clement as the third successor of Peter (Peter, Linus, Anacletus, Clement). With Clement as the successor of Peter in Rome, is then the Roman Catholic doctrine of apostolic succession (the uninterrupted series of popes from the present back to Peter) a valid doctrine? Well, Clement was certainly bishop of the Roman congregation. Of Anacletus (or Cletus, according to another tradition) and Linus we know only the names, but it is quite possible that they were also bishops of the Roman congregation. But what was a bishop at that time? The answer can only be that this office was something essentially different from what it later became.

First of all, there were several bishops holding office simultaneously, and at the beginning these bishops had purely technical functions. *Episcopos* is the Greek word for bishop; it means "overseer." To oversee the orderly course of the external affairs of the congregation was the original function of the bishops. They were assisted by deacons. At first the bishops had very little to do with the spiritual life of the congregation. Gradually spiritual tasks were entrusted to them, first as an addition to their tasks, and then exclusively. To be sure, bishops held a respected position in the congregation, but it is improper to speak of Linus, Cletus, and Clement as bishops or popes in the way the Catholic church understands those offices. That is the first point.

The second point is even more important: was Peter the first Roman bishop? This is completely out of the question. The whole doctrine of the apostolic succession breaks down at this most important point, for the conscious transmission of spiritual authority from one Roman bishop to the next did not begin until much later. The much vaunted teaching about the uninterrupted chain of popes going back to Peter, and the claims derived from it, simply do not correspond to reality.

IGNATIUS OF ANTIOCH

The Office of a Bishop

Antakya, as ancient Antioch is called today, is only a shadow of what it used to be. At one time the residence of the ruling house of the Seleucids (mentioned again and again in the books of the Maccabees), and later the capital of the Roman province of Syria, this city on the Western banks of the Orontes River has a glorious past. Here the Roman emperors built splendid edifices. In contrast to them, the buildings in which Christians worshiped were very modest. During the persecution of Diocletian these houses of worship were completely destroyed. But when Christianity later became a legal religion under Emperor Constantine churches were rebuilt, and the "golden" main church, one of the wonders of that day, was started by Constantine himself.

Antioch was the seat of a famous school of theologians, founded by the martyr Lucian. This school influenced the whole church during the fourth century. Its scholarly work on the text of the Greek New Testament was influential down through the centuries to Erasmus' edition of the New Testament which Luther used in Wartburg Castle when he translated the Bible into German. In Antioch John, surnamed Chrysostom, "the Golden Mouth" (so called because of his unique gift for preaching), was active as a pulpit orator. It was also in Antioch that Emperor Julian wrote his book *Against the Galileans,* one of the most vehement and abusive of all anti-Christian writings. Julian attempted to breathe new life into dying paganism by reopening pagan temples, a large number of which had been closed, and by fostering dormant pagan cults. His efforts were in vain, however, and he had a particular dislike for this city whose population resented not only his religious policies but also his whole personality and way of living. From Antioch Julian launched the expedition against the Persians which cost him his life.

More than thirty councils of the ancient church were held in Antioch. "Metropolis and Eye of the Christian East" was the title given to the city, and its bishop occupied a place of honor in ancient Christianity. Earthquakes and an invasion by the Persians had already devastated the city when, in the seventh century, the reign of the Muslims began. Cross and crescent fought for posses- sion of Antioch until, in the thirteenth century, the city was definitely lost to the Muslims. At the end of the fourth century Chrysostom reported that half of the two hundred thousand citizens of the city were Christians; modern Antakya has only four thousand Christians out of a total population of twenty-eight thousand.

As important as the history of Christian Antioch was in the age after Constantine, and as significant as the activity of the Antiochian school of theologians or of John Chrysostom was for the history of Christianity, the greatest significance of the city for the Christian church was in the earliest period. In an earlier chapter we spoke of that epoch when followers of Stephen gathered the first believers in Antioch, when Paul was called by Barnabas to minister there, and when the name "Christians" as such was used for the first time. Not long after, the congregation of Antioch once more experienced a time during which it was generations ahead of the development of the church in the other provinces. In fact, Antioch became the model for all other congregations. This occurred around the turn of the first century. The man to whom the congregation of Antioch owed this unique position was its bishop, Ignatius. At the time of the emperor Trajan, Ignatius energetically directed not only the Christian congregation in Antioch itself, but also congregations in the surrounding districts. It does not surprise us that he attracted the special attention of the pagan authorities. We meet him for the first time when he, like Paul before him, was taken to Rome as a prisoner. While on the journey he wrote, again following the example of Paul, seven letters to congregations of Asia Minor and to Rome. These letters are an important source of our knowledge of Ignatius himself and of the history of ancient Christianity.

Ignatius was the first to introduce the "monarchical episcopate," according to which any congregation or area could have only one bishop. Even more important was the idea that only agreement with the bishop would guarantee the purity of doctrine, and that baptism and the Lord's Supper were valid only if administered by the bishop. "He who honors the bishop, has been honored by God; he who does anything without the knowledge of the bishop is serving the devil . . . whatever the bishop approves, this is also pleasing to God" (*Letter to Smyrna,* chapters 8 and 9); one has to "obey the bishop as if he were Jesus Christ"; "everyone must show the deacons respect. They represent Jesus Christ, just as the bishop has the role of the Father, and the presbyters are like God's council and an apostolic band" (*Letter to Tralles,* chapters 2 and 3). These quotations from the letters of Ignatius (to which many more could be added) are characteristic of the views which he introduced and implemented among the congregations of Asia Minor in a variety of ways. At that time Ignatius was alone in his views; later those views became the doctrine of the Roman Catholic church and decisively influenced its understanding of what a bishop is.

What was the status of a bishop elsewhere in the ancient church at the time of Ignatius? The *Teaching of the Twelve Apostles,* a writing which dates from shortly after the letters of Ignatius and which may have been written not far from Antioch, is fairly representative of the prevalent view. This document says: "Appoint for yourselves bishops and deacons . . . , for their ministry to you is identical with that of the prophets and teachers. Therefore do not despise them" (chapter 15).

The view of the ancient church, then, was quite far removed from the views of Ignatius. In fact, it was often necessary to bolster the authority of bishops. For the early church real spiritual authority lay elsewhere: first of all in the Lord himself, then in his apostles, who served all congregations and worked as his messengers evangelizing and filling the world with his word. In the individual congregations the prophets and teachers exercised authority, not because of their office, but because they possessed the Spirit of the Lord. The offices of bishop and deacon were instituted to take care of everyday needs; these men were to attend to the secular business of the congregations, take care of the poor, and regulate the externals connected with the Lord's Supper. The number of bishops and deacons depended on the size of the congregations and the extent of the secular duties involved. It was not until later, when the earlier, first generation leadership died out, that these secular administrators, the bishops, assumed the spiritual functions in addition to secular duties. Therefore the admonition was given: "Do not despise them."

Very soon, however, this admonition was no longer needed, for the example of Ignatius had its effect. A bare century later one would have had to admonish: "Do not overestimate them." By the time of Luther the Ignatian type of episcopal office had existed for more than a thousand years and was the backbone of the Roman Catholic system. Luther did not abolish the office, as we see in the fact that there are bishops in the Lutheran churches of Europe. But just as the Protestant clergyman is something completely different from the Catholic priest, so is a Protestant bishop distinguished from a Catholic one. What does Luther say? "What, then, are the priests and bishops? Answer: Their government is not a matter of authority or power, but a service and an office, for they are neither higher nor better than other Christians." All Christians are, on the basis of the priesthood of all believers, clergymen and bishops with all privileges. Only for the sake of good order are some ordained for special service. The highest office in evangelical Christianity is the office of pastor, of shepherd; what goes beyond that is different only in service, not in rank. And, finally, it is not bishops and pastors who make the church. According to article seven of the Augsburg Confession, the church is wherever "the Gospel is taught purely and the sacraments are administered rightly."

POLYCARP OF SMYRNA

Model Martyr

Seven letters of Ignatius of Antioch, of whom we spoke in the preceding chapter, have been preserved for us. If we did not have them we would know very little about him. The reverse is the case with Polycarp, about whom we possess an abundance of reports, although all but one of his letters are lost. It is through these reports that we know of the excellent reputation which Polycarp enjoyed in the ancient church.

The only letter from his pen which has been preserved is one addressed to the congregation at Philippi, which is known to us through the New Testament as Paul's favorite congregation. The Philippians had asked Polycarp to send them all the letters of Ignatius which he had in his possession. Along with these letters he enclosed one of his own, in which, in just a few pages, he endeavored to describe for the Philippians the sum of the Christian life as he understood it.

This letter is truly astonishing, for it consists largely of quotations. Why? Did Polycarp not have anything of his own to say? Even if he was not as gifted with the pen as Ignatius, the reason for his extensive use of quotations must have been a sound one. We think that, unlike Ignatius, Polycarp was not expressing any new insights which would have had to be expressed in his own language. Rather, he was filled with the message of the apostles which had become so much a part of his life that he spoke in its words instead of his own. This was true whether he was addressing a distant congregation by letter or speaking to his own congregation in Smyrna.

Despite the extensive use of quotations (especially from the letters of Paul, but also from 1 Peter and 1 John, as well as from the letter of Clement to Corinth), Polycarp's letter is of considerable significance for us. This letter is a document from which we learn something of how the New Testament came into being; it also serves a number of apologetic purposes. Both 1 Peter and 1 John are positively referred to in this letter for the first time. If the letter of Polycarp was written between 110 and 120 (in the very last years of Ignatius' life), it proves unequivocally that the above-mentioned letters of the New Testament were not only available, but also widely circulated and very highly regarded throughout the church at that time. When the claim is made in some quarters that the letters of Paul were not really written and made a part of the New Testament until the second century or even later, we can, on the basis of Polycarp's letter, call such assertions by their right name—fantasy.

Our major interest in Polycarp's letter, however, is that it confirms what we know about Polycarp from other sources. Just as Ignatius was a representative and pioneer of new thoughts, Polycarp was a preserver of tradition. Although the church fathers Irenaeus and Tertullian called him a pupil of the apostle John, we do not know with any certainty whether he really did have personal contact with the apostles. What we do know with certainty is that Polycarp can be linked with those who, in their youth, saw the Lord himself.

In all probability Polycarp was born around A.D. 70 and died in the year 156. His long life was a bridge from the eyewitnesses of the Lord to the Christians of the second century. Irenaeus, although he was only a youth at the time, retained an indelible memory of his meeting with Polycarp in Asia Minor. Decades later Irenaeus was able to describe the appearance and habits of that venerable man; he remembered where Polycarp used to sit when he preached and lectured and the stories Polycarp used to tell about his own encounter with those who had seen the Lord. Polycarp was a respected authority, not only in his own congregation and in Asia Minor, but also in Rome, whose bishop held him in high esteem, even though that bishop made extensive claims for himself.

Shortly before the end of his life Polycarp traveled to Rome to settle a dispute concerning the observance of Easter. In Asia Minor the day of the Lord's death was commemorated on the same date each year, regardless of which day of the week it happened to be. This custom was unknown in Rome, where Easter was not specially emphasized since each Sunday was a celebration of the resurrection of the Lord. It was not until later that the Sunday following the day of the death of Jesus was distinguished as the day of Easter and that a special annual commemoration of the resurrection was observed by Rome. Polycarp and the Roman bishop came to no agreement on this matter, although the Roman bishop did agree to tolerate the customs of Christians from Asia Minor (who even in Rome celebrated the accustomed holidays), which differed from the Roman custom. A few decades later this question caused a break in church fellowship between East and West. In token of his great esteem for Polycarp the Roman bishop made his own church available for Polycarp to celebrate the Lord's Supper.

To be sure, the great respect for Polycarp was not based solely on his age and the fact that he was a link between first generation and later Christians. The real ground of his greatness was his death as a martyr. His death was the crowning event of his life. We are told about his martyrdom in some detail by a simple report written shortly after his death and passed on to other congregations by the congregation of Smyrna. According to this report the Roman proconsul and Polycarp faced each other in the arena, surrounded by a noisy crowd, which was waiting for a new victim. "Take the oath [to Caesar] and I will let you go; revile Christ," the proconsul repeatedly urged him. "For six and eighty years have I been his

[Christ's] servant, and he has done me no wrong. How can I deny my King, who saved me?" the aged Christian replied. Neither the threat of wild beasts nor of the pyre could frighten him, nor could the renewed urging of the imperial proconsul change Polycarp's mind. Thus, with the noise of the crowd ringing in his ears, he was bound to the stake and burned. A final thrust of a dagger insured his end. His remains were reduced to ashes in the hope of obliterating his memory.

In vain! Through his congregation and the tradition of centuries Polycarp's memory has been preserved, not because he wrote a letter, as many others before and after him have done; not because his life reached back to the time of the apostles; and certainly not because he played a part in the ecclesiastical disputes of his time. His memory lives because he was a witness to his Lord, one who kept faith despite all temptations, even in the face of death: "How can I deny my King, who saved me?"

SIMON THE MAGICIAN

The Struggle with Gnosticism

In the eighth chapter of Acts we read about a certain Simon the Magician. After the death of Stephen, Philip undertook a missionary journey in the course of which he came to Samaria; here his work met with much success. Among those won to Christianity was Simon, an itinerant miracle worker. He was so impressed by the powerful deeds which he saw Philip perform that he received baptism and attached himself closely to Philip. Hearing that Philip had gathered a congregation, Peter and John went to Samaria to receive the new brethren into the fellowship of the church by the laying on of hands. This act conferred upon the new Christians the Holy Spirit who manifested himself in speaking in tongues, that is, in ecstatic, enthusiastic speech. When Simon saw this he asked the apostles to grant him this power of bestowing the Holy Spirit on others, and offered them a sum of money in return. He obviously thought this would be quite an addition to his store of miraculous powers and would add to his ability to impress the pagan population which already called him "that power of God which is called Great." The apostles refused Simon's request and sharply rebuked him for his presumptuousness.

This is all that Acts tells about Simon, but there are other sources stemming from the ancient church which tell us more about him. These other sources give us a detailed account of his encounter with Peter in Rome. According to these sources Simon had won a large group of followers through the exercise of his magic; these people honored him because of the divine power they believed he possessed. Through prayer, however, Peter showed that Satan, not God, was the source of Simon's power.

This legend is part of a farfetched apocryphal story which nonetheless reveals that Simon belonged to those groups which caused the church grave concern because they mixed the Christian message with non-Christian elements. The surname given to Simon by the people according to Acts, "that power of God which is called Great," indicates that Simon belonged to a religious tradition generally known as Gnosticism. The word "Gnosticism" is derived from the Greek word for knowledge (*gnosis*) and refers particularly to knowledge about God, the world, and man which goes beyond that generally accessible to ordinary mortals. Such knowledge could supposedly unlock mysteries and reveal the secret connections between events which would otherwise remain unintelligible to the uninitiated observer.

No doubt such Gnosticism is older than Christianity. For many it offered an answer to man's age-old yearning. Before the advent of Christianity, Gnosticism had appropriated a number of elements from the various religions then prevalent and combined them into a unique mixture. Although the form in which Gnosticism found expression depended on the area of the world in which it appeared, its intent was very much the same everywhere: to provide the answer to the riddle of the world and of human existence. Not even Judaism was able to escape the influence of this movement which tended to melt all religions into one.

The attempt was also made to incorporate Christianity into the new Gnostic system. Even in the New Testament we see evidences of Gnosticism at work in Christian congregations. Colossians 2 deals with such Gnostic influence. In the opinion of many the Gospel of John betrays traces of having been influenced by Gnosticism. But all of this belongs to the earliest period of the contact between Christianity and Gnosticism; it was not until the second century that the real showdown between the two took place. At that time the church fathers vehemently opposed Gnostic tendencies in order to protect Christianity from internal destruction. Indeed, from the second century on there was a Gnosticism which could call itself Christian because it gave Christ a central position within its system. This kind of Gnosticism, if successful, would have included Christianity in that process, which had been at work for some time, of melting religions into one. So then, such church fathers as Irenaeus, Hippolytus, and others were right when they waged theological warfare against Gnosticism.

Unfortunately, the original writings of the Gnostics are no longer extant. Until the recent past all we had was what could be reconstructed from the writings of the church fathers against them. But in Egypt in 1945 some peasants discovered what proved to be a whole Gnostic library of books written on papyrus. These evidently had been buried in the sand around the end of the fourth century, shortly before Christian monasteries took over this area on the banks of the Nile. Even if all of these writings are not original writings but Coptic translations, we now have almost all the Gnostic writings used by the church fathers along with much other material.

With this discovery a new epoch in the research on Christian Gnosticism began. So far only a few of the texts have been published or even satisfactorily investigated, but we have hopes that in the not too distant future much light will be shed on the darkness which has obscured Christian Gnosticism up to now. We knew the names of various Gnostic movements, but we were not able to say with certainty just what their views were. Nor was it possible to establish the origins of these movements, how their beliefs were formed and developed, or what was the connection between them. Ancient Christian literature, which was all we had to go on until now, called Simon the Magician the ancestor of all these groups. This is why we included him in this book. Early Christian writers said that the whole Gnostic movement started with him. He in turn was supposed to have been a pupil of a certain Dositheos. This legend is hardly correct; the facts are much more complicated.

Christian Gnosticism was mainly concerned with two questions. The first was: how did evil (that is, imperfection rather than sin) come into the world? The second question was: how can man free himself from evil? If God is the highest and most perfect being—and there is no doubt about that—it is impossible for him to have created such a defective and imperfect world. Thus it was assumed from the outset that other powers were involved. This idea of other, divine powers which are subordinate to God was common to all Gnostic systems.

The highest God, according to the Gnostics, generated out of himself a series of divine beings which differed from each other in degrees. The earlier they came into being and the closer they were to God, the more they were like him; the later they were generated out of God and the more removed they were from him, the more distinct they were from the divine. The divine being who created the world was, according to the Gnostics, one of the lowest of these divine beings. Nonetheless, there was still something of the highest God in this creator, and in the mankind created by him.

Salvation in the Gnostic system depended on liberating the divine spark of the highest God from the realm of the material world and on leading it back to the highest God. That is not easy, since the Creator-God and his helpers do everything possible to keep man imprisoned in the realm of the flesh and to kill in him the memory of his ancestry from on high. Thus it is extremely important for man to keep alive the memory of his origin. If he possesses this knowledge, he can return to the realm of the highest God. In this system only the soul is important; the flesh is worthless and despicable. Therefore the soul has to be furnished with the insights and qualities which enable it to pass through the numerous heavenly worlds located between earth and the highest God. The purpose of the extensive Gnostic literature, then, was not only to instruct the believer about the origin and structure of this visible world and of the worlds above, but to furnish him—and that was the most important and complicated task—with the means whereby he could be victor over the powers of darkness.

It is Christ and the apostles who appear in many Gnostic writings to reveal these mysteries. The church countered the claims of the Gnostics by stating that nothing of this system was to be found in the Gospels, the Acts of the Apostles, and the letters of Paul, as they were used in the congregations. (The Old Testament did not come into question because it was rejected by the Gnostics as a work of the Creator God.) The Gnostics acknowledged this, but argued that such knowledge was a secret matter about which the Lord had not instructed the general public, only his most trusted disciples. For proof the Gnostics appealed to a number of "Gospels" which they themselves had written for this express purpose. These Gnostic Gospels deal especially with the period between the resurrection and the ascension of the Lord, about which the canonical Gospels of the New Testament say very little. The Gnostics also produced biographies of the apostles in which the apostles reported what the Lord had secretly communicated to them. The Gnostics asserted that the Lord's true teaching was to be seen in these writings more clearly than in the Gospels used by the church.

It was not easy for the church to defend itself against Gnosticism. Although not the only one, a most important problem for the church was to determine what really constituted a true Gospel and a genuine apostolic writing. Furthermore, the theologians of the church had to demonstrate to rank and file Christians that the Gnostic conception of God, with its system of higher and lower deities, had no place in Christianity, for it led to a devaluation of the person and the work of Christ.

Gnosticism divided Christians into various groups, depending on whether they had this secret "knowledge" or not. Those who had only the simple Christian faith and knew only the message of the New Testament were not capable of complete salvation. The Gnostics praised their own knowledge as the highest good and as the perfection of the teachings of the New Testament. Actually, however, Gnosticism was nothing else but an attempt to draw Christianity into that process of religious intermingling which was a distinctive feature of the collapse of paganism and of the ancient world.

MARCION

Apostle of the Strange God

At the end of July, A.D. 144, a hearing took place before the clergy of the congregation in Rome. This hearing was to be of great consequence for the church in the decades and centuries that lay ahead. Marcion, a Roman Christian who had come originally from Asia Minor, stood before the presbyters of the congregation to expound his teaching. So far as we know this exposition was not a defense against attack but an attempt to win the clergy and the congregation to his point of view. For some years he had been a member of the Roman congregation, evidently without causing offense; perhaps he was even quite respected. At the time he became a member of the congregation he had proved the sincerity of his faith by making a large financial contribution. Otherwise he was a very quiet member of the church in Rome.

But what he now expounded to the presbyters was so monstrous that they were utterly shocked! The hearing ended in a harsh rejection of Marcion's views. He was expelled from the Roman congregation and his gift of money was returned. The break between the church and him was complete. He had previously been expelled from his home congregation in the vicinity of the Black Sea, possibly by his own father, the bishop of the congregation of Sinope, Marcion's birthplace. From this time on Marcion went his own way and energetically advocated a strange kind of Christianity which quickly took root throughout the whole Roman Empire and became a serious threat to the mainstream Christian church. In several regions Marcion's version of Christianity competed vigorously with that of the church for supremacy. In the West the Marcionite sect persisted for nearly a century, and in the East it lingered on until the age of Constantine. But even in the West, where Marcion's views found support for only a relatively short time, the threat to orthodox teaching was considerable. For precisely in these hundred years, until the middle of the third century, new afflictions troubled the church. Various forms of Gnosticism bored at the church from within; Montanus promoted his Spirit-type Christianity; and then, too, there was steady oppression by the state.

Under these circumstances we can understand why the church opposed Marcion so vehemently. Polycarp is reported to have called him the "firstborn of Satan." But in rejecting Marcion's views, the church also rejected some legitimate concerns. It has not been until recent decades that we have been able to make a more accurate evaluation of Marcion. The great church historian Adolf von Harnack wrote a famous book on Marcion to which he gave the subtitle, "The Gospel of the Strange God." In this book Harnack argued that there were striking similarities between Luther and Marcion. Harnack regarded Marcion as a true disciple of Paul and a real reformer of the church. Marcion's work, Harnack held, was as significant for the second century church as that of the Protestant Reformers was for the church of the sixteenth century. Harnack even asked whether the line from the prophets to Jesus to Paul "is not continued rightly only in Marcion."

Just what did Marcion teach and do? How did he arrive at his teachings and demands? As far as we can deduce from the extant remnants of Marcion's works and the polemics of Christian authors against him, the complete newness that came to earth in Christ was the starting point of his thinking. Marcion saw the gospel's key issues most clearly set forth in the Letter to the Galatians and in the Letter to the Romans: "If justification were through the law, then Christ died to no purpose" (Gal. 2:21).

Christians live in and through faith, therefore the epoch of law is at an end (Gal. 3:23–25). Christ and the law are irreconcilably opposed to each other. Again and again Christ broke the law, Marcion believed, in order to show that its validity was at an end, as the reports of certain events in the Gospels prove. The Sermon on the Mount shows most clearly that the demands made upon Christians stand in pointed contrast to the principles valid in the Old Testament. The Old Testament required the righteousness of an eye for an eye, a tooth for a tooth. Christ, however, commands love even toward one's enemies (Luke 6:35) and benevolence where one could not hope to receive something in return (Luke 6:32–35).

The Old and the New Testament, Marcion argued, cannot be reconciled to each other. Any one who reads the Old Testament attentively must discover how imperfect its God is. This imperfection can be seen as early as the creation. Hardly had the Creator-God breathed life into man than he began to worry that this his creature might become a rival. Therefore, full of jealousy, he forbade man access to the tree of knowledge and of life. This God was not able to prevent one of his angels from falling away from him and leading man to disobedience. This God regretted that he had created man and expelled him from paradise. Weak and helpless, left prey to sickness and death, man now exists in this world as a true copy of the imperfection of his creator, just as the world itself is a reflection of the defectiveness of its creator. This imperfection is obvious in all creation and life, human and animal. How repulsive and infamous are the circumstances under which man is begotten and develops until he finally sees the meager light of this world! Man's end—rotting away in the earth whence he came—is worthy of his beginning.

What was life like before Christ came to earth and had mercy on man? According to Marcion, the Creator-God was able to hold men in check only by terrible threats and punishments. You have only to look at the Old Testament, Marcion said, to get a clear picture of what its "saints" were like. There is no outrage that is not committed by them, and they did it with the approval of the Creator-God! He not only forgives, he even commands his followers to deceive, rob, and commit violence against all who oppose him. It is impossible that the Creator-God whom we meet in the Old Testament is the same God who manifests himself to us in Jesus Christ. Just as the New Testament has nothing in common with the Old Testament, so also the creator of this world and the eternal, good God of love who saves men in Jesus Christ cannot have anything in common with each other. So Marcion concluded that there must be two gods: one a low God, the creator, whose book is the Old Testament and whose law is the Jewish law of retaliation, and a higher God, who is absolutely good, and who was unknown to us until he revealed himself to men in Christ.

This higher God, until that time a stranger to mankind, really had nothing to do with mankind. Man was none of his concern, for he had not created him. Nonetheless he came as Christ to the earth which was foreign to him. He turned to the poor, the desolate, and the hungry—not to the righteous who served the Creator-God and obeyed his commands. In fact, Christ came to abolish these precepts of the Creator-God. The imperfection and inadequacy of the Creator-God is seen in the fact that he was unable to prevent the coming of the good God of whose very existence he was completely ignorant.

Furthermore, this Creator-God did not understand the intent or significance of Christ's ministry. Ultimately, however, he realized that Christ's ministry meant the destruction of his kingdom. The Creator-God then incited his followers, the Jews, to crucify Christ. But instead of thwarting Christ's work in this way, the Creator-God actually helped to accomplish its fulfillment. For Christ, by dying the death of the cross, redeemed mankind from the reign of the Creator-God. Christ penetrated even into Hades and freed those who had been damned by the Creator-God as sinners. However, Christ was not able to save the righteous of the Old Testament, for they could not free themselves from the Creator-God and put their faith in Christ. Only those who are able to trust completely in the infinite love of the God who acted in Christ—and this love is valid for all men—and who surrender themselves to him in unconditional faith, are saved.

To be sure, as long as men are in the flesh (which comes from the Creator-God), they will have to suffer much, especially at the hands of those obedient to the Creator-God. Such suffering, however, is but a little matter, for the body and this world are of no account. The true Christian despises both. He disdains the care of his body and subdues it by fasting. The Christian even renounces marriage and procreation; if he is married he dissolves the marriage. To beget children is to pass on to them the fetters and the misery in which the parents languish. At the end of time the good God will summon mankind before his judgment seat, not to judge (since he himself is love), but to separate the people. Those who entrusted themselves to him in faith he will receive to himself; the others he will abandon to the Creator-God, with whom they will find their end. For this Creator-God and all his creatures are finite, whereas the good and higher God is eternal and imperishable.

This, briefly, is the teaching of Marcion so far as we can reconstruct and describe it. How was Marcion able to find his beliefs in the New Testament? He simply rejected the Old Testament as well as any revelatory writings other than the New Testament, particularly Gnostic writings. Even though Marcion held much in common with Gnosticism, he differed from it in several important respects.

If Jesus really was what Marcion portrayed him to be, how is it possible that Christ's person and teaching were corrupted within so short a time? Marcion explained this corruption on the basis of the Letter to the Galatians in which Paul emphasizes that there is only one gospel, namely, that which is proclaimed by him (Gal. 1:8–10), and states that false brethren attempt to turn the congregations from this gospel (1:6–9; 2:11). The contents of the letter inspired Marcion to declare that everything in the New Testament which did not agree with his view was a later alteration of Scripture. (For all practical purposes the New Testament of Marcion's day consisted of the four Gospels and the letters of Paul. The other parts of the New Testament were at that time not yet everywhere accepted as such.) False teachers, he said, had begun to change Jesus' message. The apostles were too weak and too imprudent to prevent this. Even during Jesus' lifetime they had failed often enough. Furthermore, they did not support Paul sufficiently in his struggle against false teachers. Thus it was possible that after the death of Paul, who was the only one who understood Jesus correctly, the apostle's letters were altered. Therefore it was necessary to purge the New Testament of later additions and alterations. Marcion undertook the purification of the Gospel of Luke and ten letters of Paul in a way calculated to support his doctrinal views.

At this point we must register an emphatic objection to Marcion. Even in the form in which Marcion edited Luke and the Pauline epistles they do not justify the doctrines he advanced. Despite all of Marcion's editing, it is obvious that for Luke and Paul the Creator-God and the father of Jesus Christ are identical, and that the Old Testament was the preparation for Jesus' coming. Marcion's concept of Jesus as well as his interpretation of Paul are products of the imagination. Even though Marcion was correct in reviving the teachings of Paul on grace and salvation—teachings which had faded in the church of the second century—the apostle Paul would have been one of Marcion's strongest adversaries.

Marcion read into the Scriptures anything that pleased him. What he presented as a solution is in the last analysis nothing but the protest of human reason against the reality of God. It is an inadmissible simplification to ascribe everything in the idea of God which is uncomfortable for us to another, lower God! Only if the Creator-God and the Savior-God are one does the concept of God have its full depth. Only when we have learned that even the needs and afflictions which we face on this earth come from the hand of that God who is infinite love and who saves us do we begin to understand God.

Marcion started out with a pessimistic world view and made his human presuppositions absolute instead of overcoming them. He did not bow to the reality of God but attempted to alter reality according to his desire and needs, and so he became increasingly entangled in error. The church learned much from the struggle against Marcion. But as important as he was for the development of the Christian church his teachings cannot be compared with those of Paul or Luther. Marcion's teachings are inferior to these by far.

MONTANUS

The Attempt to Reverse History

Marcion attempted to renew the church by restoring what he regarded as the pure teachings of Christ and Paul. Montanus, too, felt the need of restoring the church to the purity of an earlier age, and despite much opposition to Montanism, the charge of heresy was not lodged against it, at least not in the first decades of the movement. In their theological thinking Montanus and his followers evidently were not different from the church as a whole, at least not in essentials. The fact that Montanism caused widespread controversy and ultimately led to the excommunication of its adherents was due to other reasons.

In order to understand these reasons, it is necessary to visualize the condition of the church around the year 150. The early or primitive period was definitely over. Paul and the Twelve had blended, so far as most were concerned, into a unified group, and the tensions between them were forgotten. Christians were resigned to the fact that the Lord had not yet returned. First generation Christians had been firmly convinced that they would see the Last Day and they expected the end of the world at any moment. Even the fact that Christians were dying before the end came could not shake this expectation. The second generation continued in this conviction. Ignatius of Antioch declared, "The last times have come." Gradually, however, around the year 100, the change began to come. To be sure, the Epistle of Barnabas said: "Close at hand is the day." But *2 Clement* said: "Thus we do not want to despair, but want to endure in hope . . . since we do not know the day of the appearance of God."

The Shepherd of Hermas suggested a solution to the problem of the Lord's failure to come: God had delayed the return of Christ in order to give Christians the opportunity for a second repentance through which they could wash away the sins committed since their conversion. Of course, this time of penitence was seen as having a limit; but once the theory that the time of the Last Judgment had been delayed was proposed, it soon took hold and found acceptance. Gradually the idea of a limited, final opportunity for repentance faded more and more into the background, until finally the conviction gained ground that Christ's return and the day of judgment would indeed take place, but in an indefinite future.

People no longer lived as if each day might be the last but began quite unconsciously to make themselves at home in this world. Hand in hand with that went a change in the standards applied to their own actions as well as those of others. The moral demands still remained quite rigorous, but they were no longer as absolute as they had been in the first decades. Also, the structure of the congregations underwent change. The congregations founded by Paul had no real office or officials. Naturally, there were always men and women who managed congregational affairs such as caring for the poor, but these were services which grew out of an egalitarian fellowship. The form of their public worship, for instance, was determined by the working of the Spirit, who moved various people at various times to lead, pray, or prophesy. More and more the direction of the public worship and the responsibility for spiritual leadership had fallen to certain chosen individuals; the remaining members of the congregations no longer felt responsible for these matters. Offices which were restricted to certain qualified people began to take shape. Gradually measures of authority were granted to these offices or assumed by those who held them. The congregation changed from a community in which all had held equal rights into a community with differentiated rights and duties.

Many Christians, however, resisted this development. They could not resign themselves to the fact that the church had begun to feel at home in this world, and in practice, if not in principle, had lowered the rigorous moral demands of the earlier period. Nor could these Christians resign themselves to the fading expectation of Christ's return. The spirit of the primitive church still lived in them, but they had no leader to rally them and give expression to their convictions, and thus reverse the trend of the times. Then Montanus came on the scene. He was the man who rallied them and inaugurated a movement which spread over a wide area and who tried to effect a return to the spirit and forms of the primitive Christian era.

Montanus made his first appearance around the year 156 in a village in Phrygia. He spoke in tongues, as had many of the first Christians. With him were the prophetesses Maximilla and Priscilla, who also had the gift of tongues. The substance of their message was that the end of the world was at hand! The end, they said, would come before their death, but not until wars and riots plagued the world. Then the Jerusalem that would last a thousand years would come down from heaven, not in Palestine, but there in Asia Minor. They called upon all believers to gather either in Pepuza or Tymion, both small Phrygian towns, to await the end. Of course, due preparation for the end would be necessary. One had to be a serious and total Christian to withstand the coming judgment. Therefore the ecclesiastical regulations, for instance, in regard to fasting and marriage, were stringently enforced by the Montanists, as they began to be called. The Christian was required actively to seek martyrdom. There were, no doubt, still other Montanist demands similar to those about which we have definite knowledge. On the whole, their moral standards were far higher than those generally observed. They took the imminent end of the world seriously. If the Last Day is standing at the door, then everything on which man usually sets his heart is of no value.

The center of the new movement was Phrygia. But Montanism soon extended beyond the borders of this province and even of Asia

Minor. Everywhere there were Christians for whom Montanus' proclamation of the imminent end of the world was a confirmation of their own opinions and hopes.

What stand should the church take toward this new movement? At first the church was perplexed. It felt instinctively that Montanus' preaching could not be the work of the Spirit; at the same time, however, it did not have the weapons to fend off this new development. Montanus advanced the shocking claim that the Paraclete, promised by the Lord in the Gospel of John (14:16, 26; 15:26; 16:7-15) was speaking through him. The Paraclete, translated in the King James Version as *Comforter* in the sense of assistant or helper, was to bring the final revelation of the Lord (John 16:13): "he will guide you into all the truth." Montanus, therefore, demanded and supposedly deserved obedience.

The church's defense got off to a slow start. An attempt by the church to cast out the spirit at work in the two prophetesses by means of exorcism of demons failed. Then the first synods began to convene to consider countermeasures. Now the church began to resist the new movement, and it pushed out the Montanists. As a result, however, Montanism became an even more dangerous foe, for it developed into a rival or counter-church with an organization that was very tight and in many respects superior to that of the regular church.

But help came. One thing that helped was the successful attempt to prevent recognition of the Montanists by the Roman church, which had been close to conferring recognition on them. This would have complicated matters greatly. Still, important as this victory was, something else helped even more. As time went by, the Montanist prophecies went unfulfilled. The end of the world did not come and therefore resistance to the new sect became easier. Maximilla had prophesied that the end of the world would come after her death. She died, but the world continued to exist. Did this not prove the fraudulent character of the "new prophecy" as Montanism was also called?

Montanism had come into being as a reaction against the historical development of the church. Yet the same thing took place within Montanism as had taken place in the church on a greater scale. At the beginning of the movement the prophetic element had been most prominent, but it eventually died out, and the sayings of the prophets were collected in holy books which became a substitute for new oracles. In its first period Montanism claimed that it was led by the Spirit himself, who guided true believers through Montanus and his associates; later, definite offices were established in the movement. At first the belief was that the end of the world was imminent; gradually the idea of the Lord's return was pushed into the more general future. The same thing had happened within the church earlier, and, as a parallel development took place in Montanism, the church's opposition to Montanism was justified all the more.

Finally all that remained of original Montanism were the rigorous moral demands, far stricter than those of the church as a whole. It was these high moral demands that persuaded Tertullian, an outstanding early theologian, to become a Montanist. Tertullian's conversion to Montanism in the year 207 gave the movement a new thrust, but Montanism was no longer what it had been. All that remained was a moral reform movement whose original presuppositions had faded away.

Montanism was an attempt to arrest the historical development of the Christian church at a certain point. But it was, as it always is, impossible to reverse the course of history. The subsequent internal development of Montanism justified the historical development which took place in the church in the first half of the second century.

THE APOLOGISTS

Defenders of the Faith

Christianity had its beginnings in a small corner of the ancient world, and it went unnoticed for a long time by the people of rank, influence, and reputation. We may get just the opposite impression when we read the Book of Acts, but this must not deceive us. It makes a difference whether one looks at a new movement from the inside or from the outside. None of the disputes and tumults of which we read in the Book of Acts seriously affected either the state or the public of that time. As far as the authorities were concerned, Christianity was only one of many phenomena among the rabble — sometimes interesting, sometimes bothersome, but in any case simply of no great importance.

In the course of time, however, things changed. Christianity spread, not only to every province of the Roman Empire, but to every level and class of society. Christians were to be found not only among the slaves and the lower middle class, but even in the circles of the nobility and of Roman senators. Even those who had never known a Christian personally had nonetheless heard of this new sect which would not accommodate itself to being just one of the many religious fellowships of that day. It is true that the Jews rejected the veneration of the indigenous gods, but people had come to expect that of them in the course of the centuries.

The Christians, however, were a new sect, and the arrogance with which they rejected all the traditional gods and religions was regarded as most insolent. Belief in these gods, Christians held, was wrong and wicked, for God is invisible. If this had been the extent of the Christians' uniqueness, they would not have received much notice. What really gave offense was their belief that God had appeared visibly on earth in Christ, his Son. This was regarded as blasphemy, for it was known who this Christ was. He had appeared just a few decades before in Palestine, a place far off in the hinterland. This Christ came from the poorest of the poor and was ignored by all intelligent people. He had died on a cross as a criminal — the Christians said for the sin of mankind.

A sophisticated person could laugh at that if the matter were not so serious! After all, these Christians even dared to refuse to venerate the emperor, who symbolized the continuance of the Roman Empire, its peace and well-being. Moreover, Christians had no use for the temples which adorned the cities and were a source of livelihood for a great many people. Most of all, people took offense at the secretiveness of Christians. There had to be a reason for that, and certainly not a good one. It was assumed that there was something sinister going on, for Christians surrounded their teachings and views with so many secrets. Was it not said that during the hours of the night men and women together celebrated bizarre meals at which they consumed the flesh and blood, as they said, of the Christ? Certainly that must mean human flesh! They called each other brother and sister even if they were complete strangers to each other and greeted each other with a kiss and embrace. Everywhere they had secret ties to each other. And what did they pray for in those prayers, the text of which they kept so secret? Most likely they prayed for rebellion and destruction, for why did they so carefully avoid holding public offices?

For most people these strange Christians were to blame for the empire's misfortunes and troubles. Either Christians had conjured up the troubles which beset the empire, or else the gods were showing their wrath because of the new sect. Therefore, away with the Christians! "If the Tiber rises as high as the city walls, if the Nile does not send its waters up over the fields, if the heavens give no rain, if there is an earthquake, if there is famine, or pestilence, straightway the cry is: 'Throw the Christians to the lions!' " This is how the early church father Tertullian described the situation of the Christians in the first centuries.

Whether the Christians wanted to or not, they had to try to break through the wall of distrust, unreasonableness, and superstition to protect themselves against the ugly mood of the masses, who repeatedly demanded Christian blood. The reserve practiced by Christians in the past had to be given up. From the middle of the second century a new kind of Christian literature developed.

This literature appeared in Asia Minor, Greece, Palestine, Syria, Africa, and Italy, and attempted to defend Christians against the charges circulated among the masses. The authors of these writings are called Apologists. They dedicated their writings to the emperors. Typical of these dedications is one by Justin Martyr: "To the Emperor Titus Aelius Adrianus Antoninus Pius Augustus Caesar, and to his Son Verissimus the Philosopher, and to Lucius the Philosopher, the natural son of Caesar and the adopted son of Pius, a lover of learning, and to the sacred Senate, together with the whole People of the Romans, I, Justin, the son of Priscus and grandson of Bacchius, natives of Flavia Neapolis in Palestine, present this address and petition in behalf of those of all nations who are unjustly hated and wantonly abused, myself being one of them."

We do not know whether the emperors ever received or read any of the "Apologies." Nor do we know whether the Christians succeeded in getting them into the hands of the educated and influential by way of the bookshops. But the gain which the Christians themselves derived from these writings was immeasurable. For here they had at hand the kind of material they needed for their daily confrontation with non-Christians. Here was an armory of arguments with which to defend their own faith and attack that of their opponents. We owe a great deal to those apologists of the second and third centuries: Quadratus, Aristides, Ariston of Pella, Tatian, Miltiades, Apollinaris of Hierapolis, Justin, Athenagoras,

Theophilus of Antioch, Melito of Sardes, and a great many others whose names and works are not known to us. If their language lacked polish, if their theological concepts were crude, their quotations from the pagan philosophers and writers sometimes superficial, and their arguments against pagan religiosity wrong, the apologists still rendered a decisive service in their day. What they started, although it was generally disregarded by the educated Gentiles of their day, was carried on by others until a few decades later the charge that Christianity was a religion of the illiterate and of the rabble had lost its sting.

By the middle of the third century men like Cyprian of Carthage, who came from the most reputable social circles, held positions of leadership in Christian congregations. And well-educated men such as Clement of Alexandria and Origen wrote works for which even the leading representatives of pagan philosophy could not deny their esteem and respect.

JUSTIN MARTYR

Apologist and Martyr

We have already spoken of the Apologists, the men who stepped forward to defend Christianity when it was attacked, and of the accusations to which they had to give reply. The most outstanding of these apologists was Justin Martyr. In all probability he was born at the beginning of the second century in Palestine, at Shechem in Samaria. His home town was mentioned in the Bible, but the only thing it had in common with the biblical city was the location. The city had been destroyed around A.D. 70 but was later rebuilt and inhabited by Greek and Roman settlers. Justin was the son of one of these settler families.

He became a Christian in the same way as many other apologists. According to Justin's own account, his path to Christianity began with Greek philosophy. He had hoped to find in philosophy the true wisdom and knowledge of this world and the world to come, for which his soul thirsted. This was not the case. He sought out representatives of each of the philosophical schools then in vogue. He discovered that the first was completely ignorant of that which he was seeking. "He neither knew God, nor considered the knowledge of God necessary," Justin reports. Another was concerned for money and not for the intellectual advancement of his students. The third wasted all his time on incidentals. Finally, Justin thought he could find satisfaction in the philosophy of Plato. However, not Platonism but a chance meeting with an old man led to the end of his search. Their conversation turned naturally to the philosophical questions that bothered Justin, and he soon realized that all his philosophical knowledge was unable to refute the arguments advanced by this man. Everything on which Justin had based his thinking, this old man tore to shreds. When Justin asked the old man where truth really was to be found, the man directed him to the prophets of the Old Testament. Here the true source of wisdom was to be found, in word and deed, not only in prophetic knowledge and in their pointing to Christ, but also in the confirmation of truth by divinely wrought miracles. "But straightway a fire was kindled in my soul, and a passionate desire possessed me for the prophets and for those great men who are the friends of Christ. And as I weighed his [the old man's] words within me, I found that this alone was philosophy, and philosophy safe and serviceable. In this way then and for these reasons am I a true [that is, a Christian] philosopher."

This story is told in the form of a dialogue between Justin and a Jewish teacher on the subject of Judaism and Christianity. Justin saw Christianity as the only safe and useful philosophy — but was it really just a philosophy for him? On the surface the answer is yes. Clothed in the garb of a philosopher (which he did not discard even after becoming a Christian), Justin traveled throughout the world interceding for Christianity in spoken and written word. One of his writings, dedicated to the Roman emperor, has been preserved, as has the *Dialogue with Trypho the Jew*. The influence of Greek philosophy on Justin, especially of the teaching of Plato, is unmistakable.

But Justin did not stop at rebuffing the attacks of opponents; he wanted not only to defend the Christian faith but also to justify it. Philosophy was not the only reason Justin became a Christian; in his so-called *Second Apology* he himself speaks among other things of the effect which the steadfastness and martyrdom of the Christians had on him while he was still far removed from Christianity. In addition to his philosophical views, Justin expounded the full Christian faith. For him Jesus is not just a gifted philosopher but the Son of God, a person of the Trinity, the one who redeemed mankind on the cross. For him Christianity is not simply a rational doctrine but the sum of the commands of Jesus. We are indebted to Justin also for some very significant statements about the Lord's Supper and baptism. Only the two works mentioned are still extant. If we still had his other works, the ones in which he addresses himself to internal questions facing the church, much more could be said!

Justin lived as he taught. During his second stay in Rome, around 165, he was arrested along with several companions who were very likely students of his. Without wavering, he refused to deny Christianity: "It was our chief wish to endure tortures for the sake of our Lord Jesus Christ and so to be saved, because this shall become to us salvation and confidence at the more fearful and universal judgment-seat of our Lord and Savior." Along with his companions he sealed his confession of faith with a martyr's death.

THE SCILLITAN MARTYRS

History Written in Blood

Opponents of Christianity often claim that "the history of Christianity is written in blood." They have in mind the persecutions, inquisitions, and wars that have been carried out in the name of the Christian faith.

However, there is another sense in which we can say that the history of Christianity is written in blood. For centuries, beginning with the crucifixion of the Lord, every Christian stood in danger of losing his life for the sake of his faith. Stephen was the first of a long line of martyrs. Some of these martyrs were simple, ordinary people; others were the apostles themselves and well-known leaders of large congregations. Up to the beginning of the fourth century, Christians could be confronted at any moment with the question of whether they were ready to die for their faith. It was this willingness to die for the sake of the Lord which won countless new followers to Christianity. Instead of deterring converts, the execution of Christians attracted adherents and actually helped to swell their ranks. Even those sophisticates who had only a mocking smile for the words "God," "faith," and "heaven," had to ask themselves where the Christians got the strength and courage to endure the tortures of inventive executioners, and where they found the joy which enabled them even to seek death, whereas for the pagan death was the end of everything, a horrible sinking into nothingness. The statement of Tertullian, "The blood of the martyrs is the seed of the church," was confirmed a thousand times over.

Our age, too, has produced martyrs for the Christian faith. We could speak of the prisons and concentration camps of the Third Reich, in which more than a few endured torture and death for the sake of their Christian faith. We could also point to the missionaries who gladly risk life and limb for the sake of their Lord and his gospel. We could cite still other examples, for many stories of modern martyrs could be told here. But there are fewer of these modern martyrs than there were in earlier centuries, and it is to the martyrs of the early period that we give our attention here.

We have a wide range of accounts from which to select, for early Christians carefully preserved the memory of the early martyrs. The day of their death was marked on the calendar and solemnly celebrated annually. The suffering of the martyrs was held up as an example to their own congregations, neighboring congregations, and to succeeding generations. If possible, a report of their martyrdom was written for their enduring memory and read before the congregation on the anniversary of their death. This could not be done in all cases; for when persecution was widespread, striking not only at one congregation but at the congregations of a whole province or even through the Roman Empire as a whole, or when it was especially ferocious, there was often hardly time or opportunity to give decent burial to the bodies of the martyrs. At such a time little thought could be given to exact accounts of their confessions before the judges, their suffering, and their dying.

Often reports of martyrdoms were embellished and enlarged upon. This was the case especially in later times when into the mouths of the martyrs were put long speeches which rebuked their judges sharply and proclaimed the truth of the Christian faith almost in the form of sermons. Still later, legends began to develop around a kernel of truth. With such legends it is very difficult to separate fiction from truth.

On the other hand there are also reports which are so brief that one could only wish for much more detail. Among those is one concerning the martyrs of Scilli in which the post pertinent information is given in brief phrases. In all probability the author of the account began immediately after the trial to write down a rough — and therefore more impressive — draft of the events of the last hours of the martyrs.

We are told nothing of the background of the trial, nothing about the persons of the accused, and nothing about the sufferings which they had to endure until they were brought before their judge. The judge was not eager to have the prisoners executed. Use your heads, he admonished them, and you can save yourselves. Why do you want to be mixed up in this madness? What we demand of you is so simple. Renounce your faith; swear allegiance to the emperor; offer a sacrifice for his well-being! This, in essence, is what the proconsul said to these Christians. In vain. One after the other refused to deny his faith: "I am a Christian man." "I am a Christian woman." "What I am, that I wish to be." Such were their replies, even though they knew full well what the consequences would be. Everyone, both judge and accused, knew that it was a question of life and death. Then the proconsul tried intimidation, but that, too, was in vain, for the Christians replied: "We have none other to fear, save only our Lord God, who is in heaven." "Honor to Caesar as Caesar: but fear to God." The proconsul tried delay tactics: "Do you want some time to think this over?" he asked. "Take thirty days to think it over." "In such a clear-cut matter there is no need to think it over," was the answer; "we are Christians and will not deny our faith."

Seven men and five women were sentenced to death by the sword. How was the sentence received? "Speratus said: 'We give thanks to God.' Nartzalus said: 'Today we are martyrs in heaven. . . .' With one voice they said: 'Thanks be to God!' " With the praise of God on their lips they went to their death without a word of complaint or a tear.

The trial described above took place in Scilli, a town of North Africa, in the year 180. The location of the town is now unknown. We do know, however, that the town was small, as was the Christian congregation there, of which probably most of the members joyfully gave their lives on the seventeenth of July in confession of their faith. When and how Christianity came to North Africa and how many Christians there were at that time is unknown to us. Significantly, though, the first news which we have of Christianity in Africa is this report of martyrdom in Scilli. The second piece of information we have concerning the Christians in North Africa is a document written twenty-two years later. This document tells of the sacrificial death of Felicitas, Perpetua, and their companions. What was it we said at the beginning of this section? "The history of Christianity is written in blood." Indeed it is!

THE MARTYRS OF
LYONS AND VIENNE

They Prayed for Life

We do not know when or how Christianity came to Southern France. Suddenly it was there, and, as in the case of North Africa, the first we know of it is through a report of a bloody persecution of Christians. A letter written by the congregations to the Christians in Asia Minor is our source of information. Eusebius preserved the letter for us in his *Ecclesiastical History*. Here we can read in detail what their martyrdom was like. The simplicity of this firsthand report is such that no commentary is necessary.

It was the year A.D. 177. The first sign of an approaching persecution was a boycott of Christians. They were forbidden access to the market and public baths. Soon it was not safe for Christians to show themselves on the street; when they did show themselves they were attacked, insulted, and robbed by the mob. They were even arrested. But none of this weakened the faithfulness of the Christians; they only became more determined in their stand. Some of them were given a public hearing in the market place before the commandant and then were thrown into prison. When they were finally brought before the governor, he threatened and beat them. One of the audience, a respected citizen, shouted a demand that the Christians be given a just hearing and the opportunity to offer a defense. The crowd shouted him down, and the governor, ignoring this demand, asked only: "Are you a Christian?" When the man replied loudly and affirmatively, he was placed under arrest.

Ten of the accused Christians suffered so terribly during their imprisonment that under the threats of death they denied their Lord. How did the congregation react? Did it grieve for the faithful who were about to die? No, it grieved rather for those who renounced the faith: "They caused us great grief and sorrow beyond measure, impairing the zeal of the others who had not been arrested. Yet they, although suffering all the terrors, nevertheless continued constantly with the martyrs and did not forsake them. But at that point we were all greatly terrified by uncertainty as to their confession, not because we were afraid of the punishments to be endured, but because we looked at the end and were afraid that some of them might fall away."

But the persecution had just begun. The number of arrests increased until all the leaders of the two congregations were in prison. The governor issued a special decree that Christians were to be sought out. Even pagan servants of Christians were arrested. The fear of the torture which they saw the Christians endure evoked from these servants the kind of confessions which the authorities desired and needed. The old slanders against Christians were revived and the public once more was inflamed against the reviled sect. Torture was widely employed, for it was now believed that there was a moral justification for such a measure. Men and women were arbitrarily subjected to torture. Here we give two examples: Blandina, a slave, and Sanctus, a deacon from Vienne.

"While we were all afraid, and her human mistress, who was herself one of the witnesses, was in distress lest the slave girl Blandina not be able, because of the weakness of her body, to make a bold confession of her faith, Blandina was filled with such power that those who took turns torturing her in every way from morning until evening, became weakened and tired. Her torturers admitted that they were beaten, for they had nothing left to do to her, and they marvelled that she lived through it, seeing that her whole body was mangled and broken. And they testified that any one of these tortures was sufficient to destroy life, not to mention many tortures. But the blessed woman, like a noble athlete, renewed her strength in her confession of faith, and she found comfort and rest and freedom from the pain of her suffering by saying, 'I am a Christian woman and nothing vile is done by us.'

"Sanctus, too, endured nobly, beyond measure or human power, all the ill-treatment of men. The wicked hoped by persistent and rigorous torture to wring from him the confession of something unbecoming to a Christian, but he resisted them with such constancy that he would not even tell his own name, or the race or the city whence he came, nor whether he was slave or free. To all their questions he answered in Latin, 'I am a Christian.' This he said instead of giving his name or city or race or anything else. The heathen heard no other sound from him. For this reason the governor and the torturers were very eager to subdue him, so that when they had nothing left at all to do to him, they at last fastened plates of heated brass to the most tender parts of his body. His limbs were burned, but he remained unyielding and firm in his confession of faith, refreshed and strengthened by the heavenly spring of the water of life which proceeds from the body of Christ. His small body was a witness to his treatment; it was all one wound and bruise, wrenched and torn out of human shape."

The tortures were in vain. Those who had been tortured were thrown into a dark prison and subjected to new tortures; quite a few of them died of suffocation. When the bishop, Pothinus, who was over ninety, was dragged before the judgment-seat, the mob attacked him, and the governor did not intervene. "Those standing near him abused him with feet and hands and in every way, without any regard for his old age, and those who stood at a distance threw at him whatever they had at hand. . . . And he was thrown into prison, scarcely breathing, and after two days yielded up the ghost."

So the persecution raged. Even those who at the beginning had denied their Christianity, were now deeply moved. They, too, were taken to prison, where, in addition to the physical tortures, the memory of their denial tormented them. Their example encouraged the still wavering to stand fast. Now no one felt the temptation to fall away. All who were now arrested remained steadfast and went joyfully to their fate. Some were thrown to wild beasts, others beheaded, and still others were roasted to death on a red-hot iron chair set up in the middle of the arena.

Those who died in prison before they could be herded into the arena to entertain the mob were given to the dogs to eat. The bodies of the others were left to lie in the open for six days and carefully guarded so that the Christians could not bury them, even secretly. The corpses were then thrown onto a pile and burned. The ashes were scattered over the Rhone river as a final insult to the dead, for how could there be a resurrection of the body, in which the Christians believed, if nothing were left of the body?

What was left of the congregation when the persecution came to an end? A large part of its membership had died a painful death. Some had lived through the tortures, "though they had confessed their faith not once or twice, but many times, and had been taken back from the beasts and were covered with burns and scars and wounds." Were they broken and, as the saying goes today, "cured for the rest of their life"? Did they crawl into a corner so as never again to attract attention? No! When the persecution ended, the congregation rose to new heights. Irenaeus, who had been a presbyter of the church of Lyons during the persecution, became its new bishop. Under him Lyons became a theological center of the Western church. How did the Christians feel toward their persecutors and those brethren who did not stand the test? Our report has something to say about this too: "They humbled themselves under the mighty hand of God. . . . At that time they made defence for all men, against none did they bring accusation, . . . and they prayed for those who had inflicted cruelty upon them. . . . They did not boast over the fallen . . . shedding many tears on their account before the Father, they prayed for life, and he gave it to them. . . ."

IRENAEUS

Guaranteeing the Faith

Irenaeus was absent from the city of Lyons when the persecution there reached its zenith. It seems he had been sent to Rome to represent the Gallic churches, probably in the matter of the recognition of Montanism. Perhaps Irenaeus was supposed to recommend a friendly attitude toward the followers of the new movement, for the Gallic congregations were strongly influenced by currents from Asia Minor. In any case, Rome did not recognize the Montanism, as Irenaeus may have advocated. Tertullian claimed that Rome's rejection of Montanism was due to Praxeas, a man who had come to Rome from Asia Minor and who had a first hand knowledge of what Montanism was like. His reports stressed the dangers of Montanism and won Rome over to the attitude of the church of Asia Minor. Because of Praxeas' stand Tertullian hated him long after he was dead.

Evidently Irenaeus stayed in Rome for just a short time. Soon after the end of the persecution we find him in Lyons as the successor of Bishop Pothinus. We know very little about his career as a bishop. A later writer claimed that within a short time Irenaeus succeeded in converting Lyons completely to Christianity. This definitely is an overstatement, although the report certainly contains a kernel of truth, for Irenaeus had a tremendous influence on the spread of Christianity in Gaul. About the year 190 we hear once more about Irenaeus. He had written to Bishop Victor of

Rome to persuade him to adopt a more judicious attitude toward the churches of Asia Minor in the disputes over the date of Easter. From that point on we hear no more about Irenaeus. When and how he died is unknown to us. Jerome and others claim that he died as a martyr, but there is no certainty about this.

We also know very little about the youth of Irenaeus. He often recounted that in his younger years he sat at the feet of Polycarp. But that is all we know. He was probably born around 130, most likely in or near Smyrna in Asia Minor. How long he remained there and what took him to Gaul we cannot say. We know Irenaeus only from his writings, although they have not been transmitted to us in their entirety. His main work, *The Refutation and Overthrow of Knowledge Falsely So Called,* has been preserved in the Greek original in fragments and only in the Latin translation in its entirety. Another writing, *The Demonstration of the Apostolic Teaching,* has been available to us only since the beginning of this century when an Armenian translation was discovered. Until that time only its title was known.

Yet we can make some rather exact statements about Irenaeus and his significance. He was one of the authoritative representatives of a certain stage of the church's development, and this is our subject here. At the end of the second century the church succeeded in overcoming the internal crisis which had plagued it for generations. As a rule, the congregations had not been able to cope with the difficult questions put to them by the various Gnostic groups, Marcion, and Montanism. Thus there were deep-seated disagreements within the church, and large counter-churches had come into being. Although there was general agreement about rejecting these counter-churches and movements, there was no certainty about how the church was to defend or define itself against these opponents. Only gradually did the church develop certain counter-measures to protect itself, and it was during the era of Irenaeus that these measures were brought into a unified system.

Gnosticism had produced an immense number of new so-called Gospels and Acts of the Apostles. Montanus and his prophetesses had claimed that their teachings were a revelation which brought the message of Jesus to its conclusion and therefore had a higher authority than anything in our New Testament Gospels. Therefore the church began to sift critically all the writings which were circulating among the congregations: reports about the life and ministry of Jesus (that is, Gospels) and of the apostles (that is, Acts of the Apostles) and apostolic letters and revelations (that is, Apocalypses). At the same time everything which was written after the apostolic era or which proved unacceptable for reasons of content was rejected. This was the origin of the so-called canon of the New Testament, that is, a list of New Testament writings recognized by the church. But at that time the list did not yet include all twenty-seven books of our New Testament. It took almost another two hundred years until all of these twenty-seven writings were recognized and accepted throughout the church. There were long debates about several of them, but essentially the New Testament as we know it was completed by the year 200.

The development of such a list or canon was a decisive step. Its chief significance, however, was on the inner-ecclesiastical level, for it helped the church to distinguish itself from its opponents. But the controversy with opponents and splinter groups could not be continued on the basis of Scripture alone, for Scripture did not give an answer to all questions. Furthermore, Scripture could be interpreted differently, depending on the point of view from which the interpreter approached it. Besides, the followers of Marcion and the Gnostics rejected the Old Testament. Tertullian stated explicitly that it was impossible to argue with the groups separated from the church on the basis of Scripture; in fact, one should avoid such discussions, for the outsiders should not even be granted the right to appeal to Scripture.

So then a second authority was needed which could make possible a clear and unambiguous decision on the controversial questions at issue in that day. Such an authority was found in the "Rule of Faith" or the "Rule of Truth," as it was often called. This "Rule" was the confession in which the faith was summarized in concise

and generally understandable formulae. Every word of the confession of faith which constituted the "Rule" reminded the Christian of his baptismal instruction and of the teaching of the church.
Thus, the "Rule" became the fixed standard of what constituted
Christian faith. This faith, it was held, was the same as that which
had been proclaimed by the Lord to the apostles, and from the
apostles to the present in a solid line of tradition. The congregations of the true Christian church could rely on the fact that
from the very beginning of Christianity one bishop always passed
on the true doctrine to his successor. The sects and counter-churches
could not make such a claim because they had come into being only
in the recent past, and for that reason they and their teachings were
to be rejected.

Thus the bishop became the unique guarantor and guardian of
the pure faith. His position and the respect given him increased
accordingly. Naturally, the Roman bishop was especially benefitted
by this development. For if Peter and Paul had ministered there,
then the Roman church had to have an especially secure tradition,
and therefore the Roman bishop was looked upon as holding an
especially important position. Accordingly we read in Irenaeus:
"It would be very long in such a volume as this to enumerate the
successions of all the churches. However, I can point out the
tradition which that very great, oldest, and well-known church,
founded and established at Rome by those two most glorious
apostles Peter and Paul, received from the apostles, and its faith
known among men, which comes down to us through the successions of the bishops. . . . For every church must be in harmony
with this church because of its outstanding pre-eminence, that is,
the faithful from everywhere, since the apostolic tradition is
preserved in it by those from everywhere."

At that time, toward the end of the second century, the formation of the early Catholic church was completed. The congregation
of the first Christians, ruled by the spirit of the Lord, had become
a church in which the literature that was to be recognized as sacred
and the correct faith were defined by solid norms. In this way the

church gained the strength to defend itself against the disrupting tendencies in its own ranks and the various forms of crisis which appeared in the second century. Through the doctrine of apostolic succession and the emphasis on the bishop's office, the church started on a road which ultimately led to the Reformation controversies of the sixteenth century.

CELSUS

Serious Pagan Criticism

In the early period of Christianity the educated Gentile took no notice of Christians unless he was an official of the state who received complaints from citizens or information from the police and was forced, because he held public office, to deal with this curious group of people who for some incomprehensible reason refused to honor the emperor as God. But even such officials did not deal with Christians any more than absolutely necessary. If Christians sacrificed to the emperor they were released; if they refused to comply with the demands of the state, they were executed. Only rarely was an attempt made to find out what this sect was all about. The stories told about it were sufficient to form a judgment. When Pliny the Younger was governor of Bithynia, he investigated the teachings and life of the Christians. But he soon gave up his investigation out of disgust with the "eccentric immense superstition" of these people.

It soon became obvious that this attitude was not effective. Strangely enough, the Christians did not die out, although the state did its best to extinguish them by means of persecutions. Nor could the problem be solved with the slogan "there is no end to stupid people," for from generation to generation there was an increase not only in the number of Christians, but also in the number of educated people who became identified with the Christian religion either by embracing it directly or by their open sympathy with it. Something had to be done about this.

So, toward the end of the second century, we find the first pagan polemical writings against Christianity beginning to be published. Lucian of Samosata mocked Christians in his *The Death of Peregrinus*. Fronto of Cirta also dipped his pen in acid against Christians. Both attacks had only a limited effect, for the satire of Lucian did not spare paganism either, and Fronto had nothing original to offer. More was needed if the spread of Christianity was to be halted. About the year 178 the Neoplatonist philosopher Celsus wrote his *True Discourse*. Then a century later Porphyry once more attempted in his fifteen books *Against the Christians* to make a scholarly attack on Christianity.

The writings of Celsus and Porphyry summarized what pagan intellectualism could cite against the Christian faith. Certainly those two were not the only ones who did literary battle against Christianity. We know, for instance, that Hierocles, the governor of Egypt, did the same. Even crowned heads attempted to earn literary laurels in the battle against the Christians. Emperor Julian himself wrote a three volume work *Against the Christians*. But probably none of these can compare with the writings of Celsus and Porphyry. It was from these writings that Hierocles and Julian largely drew their arguments. Quite possibly other pagan writers did the same. Naturally, each literary foe of Christianity added something of his own. For example, Hierocles pointed out that Jesus was not at all unique and that Apollonius of Tyana performed similar deeds. Julian spiced his expositions with a personal passion. But they did not materially go beyond Celsus and Porphyry, who presented the objections of late antiquity to Christianity in a classical fashion.

Many people think that really dangerous literary attacks against Christianity did not begin until the period of the Enlightenment, that it has been only in the last few centuries that human reason has produced arguments which undermine faith. We think immediately of the nineteenth-century freethinkers who seduced many with their anti-Christian propaganda. In comparison with them it seems that the anti-Christian arguments of earlier periods were harmless. But this is erroneous thinking. If we look at the arguments of Celsus and Porphyry we will see that these early attacks on Christianity had an explosive power.

To illustrate this we need only look at what Celsus and Porphyry had to say about the New Testament. In doing this we have to depend on fragments of their works, for the originals of their writings are lost. Fortunately Origen wrote a reply to *The True Discourse* of Celsus in which Celsus is quoted in such detail that we can, at least approximately, reconstruct his writing. With the work of Porphyry, however, the matter is worse. We only have a series of scattered fragments which the historian Adolf von Harnack collected with painstaking care. However, his anti-Christian arguments have been quite well preserved by the fourth-century Christian author, Macarius Magnes, who quoted Porphyry's works extensively in one of his polemical writings.

The Gospel of Jesus Christ, says Celsus, which originally could have been only one, for there can be only one appropriate representation of the events, soon appeared in three, four—in fact, many—versions, so that the opponents of Christianity would no longer have a solid target for their criticism. For the more the Gospel reports vary, the more possibilities for evasion exist. The Evangelists in general have been "inventors, not reporters" of the history of Jesus, according to Porphyry. This can be proved emphatically in the case of the report about Jesus' death. If one compares the narratives of Jesus' death in the four Gospels, it can be shown that they disagree completely in details, and if they could not even report exactly the most important event in the life of Jesus, "then they also were not reliable about the others." If Christ really rose after his death, why did he appear only to a few insignificant followers, and not to Pilate, who had sentenced him, or to Herod, or at least to the High Priest? Had Jesus done that he would have proved his divinity; but as it is, the suspicion is only strengthened that the reports of the resurrection are simply products of the imagination of the disciples.

As for the Christian assertion that Jesus was predicted in the Old Testament, Celsus says that it is more than artificial to apply these Old Testament predictions to him. These passages could fit others just as well, if not better. Furthermore, the genealogies of the Gospels do not agree with each other. There are also a host of other improbabilities reported in the Gospels. In the story of the Gerasene demoniac, for instance (Mark 5:1-13), it is asserted that Jesus drove the demons from the demoniac into a herd of about two thousand swine which then drowned in the lake. How could there be such a large herd of swine in a country where the pig was considered impure and therefore abhorred? In the Gospels (Matt. 14:22-33; Mark 6:45-52; John 6:16-21) it is reported that Jesus was walking on the Sea of Tiberias when the disciples were threatened by a storm. How could Mark say such a thing when in reality this "Sea" was a "puddle" . . . which did not offer any possibility for either waves or storms.

So the attacks go on in similar fashion. The reports of the Gospels and of the rest of the New Testament are subjected to a relentless critical scrutiny. This scrutiny does not stop even at the person of Jesus (although Jesus' historicity is never called into doubt). The disciples, too, especially Peter and Paul, are submitted to a merciless scrutiny. In these critiques we see early Christianity from the standpoint of its opponents, and this perspective exerted a considerable influence on those who read this kind of literature. If the available fragments of the writings of Celsus and Porphyry were published in modern language, one could easily get the impression that these are modern authors, not writers of the second and third centuries who are joining in battle against Christianity.

Actually, these two authors presented insights which are now accepted as valid. For example, Porphyry stated that the book of Daniel did not come into existence until a very late date, a fact which was not recognized by biblical scholarship until centuries later. He said many similar things which would shock members of our congregations as inventions of "liberal scholarship." The fact of the matter is that the critical objections against certain biblical reports are almost as old as Christianity itself. We do not refute such criticisms by pretending that they do not exist. Present-day theological scholarship is not acting disrespectfully when it investigates certain human features in the Bible; it renders the church a valuable service. Such investigation shows that the church does not have to be afraid of these things. They are accessories which belong to the human history of the Bible and do not change the essence or message of the Bible. It is the fault of the theologians that this insight was not communicated in time to the church as a whole; if it had been, many a crisis and much defection during past generations could have been avoided.

CLEMENT OF ALEXANDRIA

The Christian Scholar

Today Christians are a minority in Egypt, struggling for their existence among an overwhelmingly Muslim population. They are without influence in the circles of the educated and powerful, and they live practically in hiding.

It was not always so. By the middle of the fourth century, Egypt was one of the most important centers of the Christian church, and Alexandria, its capital, was an episcopal seat which was second in renown only to Rome. Christians from everywhere came to admire the monks of the Egyptian desert and to learn from them how to lead a saintly life by mortifying the flesh and holding the world in contempt. As late as the fifth century, Alexandria rivaled Constantinople for superiority in the church of the East. For centuries the eyes of theologians were directed to Egypt.

With the onset of Islam in the first half of the seventh century all this came to an end. Alexandria was eclipsed by Constantinople. More than one hundred and fifty years of bitter internal controversies had sapped the strength of the church. At first the advancing Muslim armies were greeted as liberators. But soon suppression and persecution under the Muslims became the order of the day. The internally weakened Egyptian church was not able to cope with this situation and collapsed. The number of Christians decreased steadily, particularly among the ranks of the influential and educated. Organized Christianity survived only among the simple, stalwart country people.

So it is that a church can sink from a proud height. One thinks here of Luther's remark that God's grace is a traveling cloudburst. No church, however strong, secure, and prominent, can be certain that the judgment of God will not befall it. The church of Egypt was not the only one to succumb to the assault of Islam; the same fate befell the church of Africa. This had happened to other flourishing churches before them, beginning with those congregations in northern Asia Minor to which Paul once wrote the Epistle to the Galatians.

The collapse of these churches can serve as a warning for our day. The history of these churches reveals that they shared many common features. For one thing, the leaders of the churches were ambitious and greedy for both religious and secular power and authority. For another, the theologians engaged in dogmatism and doctrinal hairsplitting. The inevitable result was that the members of the churches became spiritually lax. But what the historian finds does not completely explain the downfall of those churches, for others with the same signs of decay did not perish. The reason these other churches survived can be grasped (not explained) only when we realize that it is not only men who are at work in history.

We do not know much about the Egyptian church before the year 200. Christianity had taken root there much earlier. Legend has it that Mark the Evangelist had done missionary work in Egypt. This, however, is very doubtful, and even the fact that Apollos of Alexandria is mentioned in Acts is not sufficient proof that Christian churches existed in Egypt at such an early date. But there definitely were Christians in Egypt around the year 125. This is proved by a famous fragment of the Gospel of John which came to light a quarter of a century ago. This fragment comes from Egypt (as do, by the way, all known major New Testament manuscripts of the early period), and it represents not only the oldest extant manuscript of the New Testament but also the oldest document of Christianity in Egypt.

Perhaps the reason we know so little about Egyptian Christianity is because it was heavily influenced by Gnosticism and because the churches in other nations did not show any particular interest in congregations outside the mainstream of the church. Gnostic predominance appears to have waned around the end of the second century. Demetrius (189-231) is the first bishop of Egypt of whom we know, and Clement the first theologian. Both were active in Alexandria, the second largest city of the Mediterranean world— Rome was the largest—and the economic and intellectual center of the nation. Here the wealth of Egypt was concentrated, and scholars came great distances to work in the city's libraries, which were unequalled anywhere in the world. Anyone who achieved a measure of success or prominence here was known throughout the nation.

Our factual knowledge about Demetrius and Clement is rather sketchy. Demetrius seems to have been responsible for the unique structure of the Egyptian church, according to which the Alexandrian bishop was the undisputed ruler of the church in his country except for the congregations of Alexandria which retained a certain degree of autonomy and independence. He was the first of a long line of princes of the church.

We know neither the year of the birth of Titus Flavius Clement (as he was known formally) nor that of his death. In all probability he came from Athens and his parents were Roman citizens. He may have left his homeland as a young man to seek wisdom in distant lands. Finally, in Egypt, he found the teacher whose knowledge and personality greatly impressed him. That teacher was Pantaenus, of whom we know little more than the name. He was the director of the catechetical school (that term meant something different from what we mean by it today) of Alexandria. Clement became his successor at the school. It was he who made this Christian school, at that time probably still a rather young institution, famous far beyond the borders of Egypt. He worked there for approximately two decades, until the persecution which broke out under Emperor Septimius Severus (202/203) forced him to leave Alexandria. From then on his trail is lost to us until ten years later when we hear once more of him in a letter written from Asia Minor which he brought to Antioch. He probably died soon after.

The major works of Clement have been preserved, and on these his fame as a Christian theologian rests. The first is addressed to the Gentiles; in it he seeks to present to them the greatness of the Christian faith and to prepare the way for their conversion. The second one is an exposition of the true Christian life, written for Christians. And the third surviving writing is a deeper treatment of Christianity for those who have acknowledged its basic features. Clement was concerned with knowledge (*gnosis,* in Greek), true Christian knowledge, not a *gnosis* which exalts itself above the faith of the congregation, the Old and New Testaments, and not a *gnosis* which separates from the church, as the other Gnostic schools did.

Clement strove to reconcile philosophy and faith. That was not a simple task, for because of the influence of those Gnostic sects which had separated from the church, the Christians of this time simply rejected philosophy outright. Indeed, the Apologists, of whom we spoke earlier, had tried to develop a "Christian Philosophy," but their efforts were only fragmentary.

Only Clement of Alexandria succeeded in reconciling and fusing Christian faith and the knowledge of that time with each other. Christianity, until then a religion of the foolish and low (1 Cor. 1:26-30), now faced the Gentile world equipped with all the weapons of contemporary scholarship. Thus a decisive step forward had been taken, but at the same time a development with grave consequences had been set in motion. This double result is seen with particular clarity in the case of Clement's successor, Origen, who surpassed Clement by far. But Origen was condemned by the church, whereas Clement pursued his work unmolested.

ORIGEN

Controversial Theologian

"It seems that most Christians are like the companions of Ulysses . . . stopping their ears with ignorance since they know that after lending their ears to Hellenic studies they will never be able to retrace their steps." This is what Clement of Alexandria wrote in one of his books. Both he and Origen opened their ears and their hearts and minds to Greek philosophy. They believed that this philosophy had a definite place in God's plan for mankind. What the Old Testament law was for the Jews, philosophy was for the Greeks. Both lead mankind to Christ.

That was the basic conviction of Clement of Alexandria. And Origen followed in his wake. Faith is the common possession of all, but it is only the first step on the way for the Christian. In baptism all receive the Holy Spirit; the Spirit works faith which leads the believer to salvation. Thus all Christians are fundamentally equal: those who have only faith and those who, in addition, possess *gnosis* (knowledge). Clement held that *gnosis* deepens that which is given in faith: "Faith is . . . a comprehensive knowledge of the essentials; and knowledge (*gnosis*) is the strong and sure demonstration of what is received by faith, built upon faith by the Lord's teaching, conveying [the soul] on to infallibility, science, and comprehension. By starting from this faith, and being developed by it through the grace of God, the knowledge respecting Him is to be acquired as far as possible." Whoever possesses this knowledge of God, the true *gnosis,* has a completely different understanding of Christianity. He is no longer ruled by fear of punishment and hope of reward in the hereafter, but solely by the love of God. The highest goal of the true Gnostic is to become like God through constantly expanded and deepened knowledge.

Origen went even further. According to him all men have within them a tiny spark of the divine light. Originally all beings participated in the deity, but they made wrong use of their free will and turned away from the divine. For this sin they were given a body. The greater their sin, the more deeply they were imprisoned in the material world. This theory accounted for the origin of the world and life. According to this view all of the imprisoned sparks retained the memory of their original existence and they all strive to regain their original state. To help them in their struggle God sends instruction into the world in various ways. Thus, the way back to God leads through a knowledge of self and a turning to virtue.

The philosophers, however, followed the divine call only partially. The Jews were given the Old Testament as a special grace of God. But all of this was not able to change mankind. Men remained in their sins until God sent the Logos, his own Son. This Logos, a part of the divine being, united himself with the pure soul of a man, Jesus. More and more this human soul Jesus was purified and drawn upward into a union with the Logos which came down until after the resurrection the two became completely one and entered again into God. This was the course of salvation appointed for all men. They must go the same way as Jesus. Completely dedicated to Jesus' example and teachings, men strive after the pure love of God and liberation from the material world. If that is achieved, they follow Jesus Christ and enter into the deity until all creation, following the unrelenting and loving call of God, has returned to him and the original condition is restored. But this restoration of the original state is not the end. Having returned to God, the emancipated spirits once more have unlimited free will, and once more they fall away from God. A new world begins and the drama begins anew, repeating itself over and over.

From this brief survey of Origen's doctrinal system the reader can understand why Christians of the second century were right in their concern about those who lent their ears to Greek philosophy. Origen was enamored of Greek philosophy, and he was led astray by its siren song. Let us recall for a moment the center of the Christian faith: Jesus' death on the cross for our sins. For Origen the death of Jesus was of minor significance — so minor that it did not even have a place in his theology. Rather, he believed that salvation is effected by knowledge: the more knowledge man possesses, the closer he is to God.

But Origen cannot be lightly dismissed. Luther condemned him sharply. Nearly a thousand years before Luther the Orthodox and the Catholic churches condemned him. Nonetheless Origen cannot simply be stricken from the history of the Christian church. It was he who helped to give Christian theology the shape it has taken through the centuries. Clement of Alexandria and Origen were the fathers of what we call scientific theology. Their way of thinking and working has had a decisive influence on theology during subsequent centuries. And the results of the theological work done during those centuries are part and parcel of the faith and teaching of all Christian churches.

Origen was without doubt the greatest theologian of the Greek church; so far as the depth, breadth, and outreach of his work are concerned he has no equal. His literary output numbers thousands of manuscripts, some quite voluminous. (Strange to say, he never wanted to be a writer, but a teacher.) He expounded all the books of the Bible either in scholarly commentaries or in sermons. The first systematic exposition of Christian doctrine came from his pen. He was one of the men to whom we are indebted for the establishment and preservation of the text of the Old Testament. In addition he was also an apologist for Christianity.

The name Adamantios, "Man of Steel," which was given Origen by his disciple Eusebius of Caesarea, seems quite appropriate in light of his life. We hear of Origen for the first time in the year in which Clement left Alexandria. It was a time of persecution. Leonides, Origen's father, was among those who had been thrown into prison. Origen at the time was not yet seventeen years of age, yet he yearned to share the fate of those who witnessed to the faith. His mother prevented him from surrendering himself to the judges only by hiding his clothes. Unable to leave the house, he tried to comfort his father by writing a letter in which he urged him not to worry about the family, but to remain steadfast before the judges. The father sealed his faith by dying as a martyr, and his worldly goods were confiscated by the state. Origen's mother, along with her seven children, was left without support.

Origen at first found a place as a foster son in the home of a rich woman, but soon he became financially independent; for despite his youth he was so far advanced in his studies that he was able to earn his living by teaching. The persecution had caused the suspension of the catechetical school in Alexandria (like Clement, other teachers also must have left the city). People interested in Christianity soon began to turn to Origen, the Christian teacher, for instruction. The number of such pupils increased. Bishop Demetrius gave his consent, and the catechetical school was resumed with the eighteen-year-old Origen as its director!

He proved himself a worthy successor of Clement. The number of students enrolled in the catechetical school increased steadily. In order to do justice to the demands made of him, he gave up his work as a grammar instructor, by which he had supported himself and devoted himself completely to teaching Christianity. He sold his collection of the works of ancient writers for an annuity which yielded enough for him to subsist. Finances would have been no problem for Origen, for his disciples would have counted it an honor to support him. Such an arrangement, however, would have gone against his ideal of apostolic poverty and the faithful obedience to the gospel for which Origen strove. He took Matthew 19:12 quite literally and owned only one coat, went barefoot, slept on the floor, ate and drank abstemiously. All of this he did in order to discipline his body as much as possible. Besides that there was his restless working for and intrepid witness to Christianity. Is it surprising that disciples flocked to this man?

Origen's scholarship was generally recognized and respected even by non-Christians. His fame spread far beyond Alexandria. Honors were increasingly heaped upon him. Not only did foreign bishops invite him to visit them, but even the imperial governor of Arabia commanded his presence in order to meet him. Origen's prestige seems to have aroused the jealousy of Bishop Demetrius. The break between the two men came when Origen, while on a journey, was consecrated a clergyman (presbyter) by friendly bishops in Caesarea in Palestine. Origen was forced to leave Alexandria around 230, but found a new home in Caesarea and there enjoyed the same acclaim he had earlier enjoyed in Alexandria. His disciple and assistant Heraclas took over the direction of the catechetical school and was later elected bishop, succeeding Demetrius. His election indicates that the break between Origen and Demetrius was probably a personal, not a disciplinary or theological matter.

Origen had been active in Caesarea for a little more than twenty years when a new persecution broke out. Naturally, special attempts were made to persuade the famous scholar to defect from Christianity. He was imprisoned and tortured with ingenious cruelty, but to no avail! Although nearly seventy years of age, Origen not only refused to defect, he admonished his friends to steadfastness. Soon after being released from prison he died, in 253 or 254, having achieved in his old age the goal which he had longed to attain in his youth.

The church has condemned Origen because of his theological views. If it had not been for these views he undoubtedly would have been canonized. And rightly so. His desire was to serve Christ with all dedication, in his scholarship as well as in his life. Even though his theology was highly controversial, there can be no doubt that Origen was a disciple of the Lord, without equal in the history of the church.

CALIXTUS OF ROME

The Church Is for Sinners

In looking at the papacy of the high Middle Ages, one might think that it was always that way. Not so at all! Only gradually did the bishop of Rome become the ruler of the Catholic church. Early in Christian history Italy played no role of any particular significance. As far as theology went, Italy's significance was far outstripped by Asia Minor during the second century and by Egypt in the third century. Palestine, Syria, and Africa also played an important role in theology, but not Italy and Rome.

As late as the early Middle Ages Rome could not claim as its own a single theologian of any renown with the exception of Hippolytus and Novatian, both of whom Rome had excommunicated. To be sure, many an outstanding theologian taught in Rome, for example, Justin Martyr, the second century apologist. But he was not a Roman; he was simply attracted to the great metropolis.

Rome's later significance was due to its geographic location; it was the capital of the empire, the place where important decisions were made. Distinguished by the activity of the apostles Peter and Paul, Rome could also boast of an important church tradition. And most important of all was the fact that the leaders of the Roman church were men with a gift for ecclesiastical organization, men who step by step established Rome's supremacy in the church.

But the material out of which Rome's supremacy was built was not fashioned by Romans. The idea of the monarchical episcopate, that is, the emphasis on the unique leadership and role of the bishop, was contributed by Ignatius of Antioch. Not even the idea that the Roman bishop was entitled to a superior rank among the bishops because he was supposed to be the successor of Peter, had its origin in Rome; Cyprian of Carthage can be thanked for this idea. But once these ideas were coined and given currency, the Roman bishops were quick to exploit them to their own advantage. Yet it would be wrong to say that Rome's bishops intentionally strove for primacy in the leadership of the church. This claim of primacy was an almost natural concomitant of Rome's geographical centrality.

The Roman claim of primacy was made with increasing emphasis until finally Leo I (440-461) stated boldly: "Through the prince of the apostles, Peter, the holy Roman church possesses supremacy over all the churches of the whole earth." With this statement the claim of the Roman papacy to supremacy reached its peak. All that was needed was the men to translate theory into reality. The centuries that followed produced such men, the kind of men who could enable the papacy to challenge the rulers of the world. The German Emperor Henry IV had to bow in penance before Gregory VII (1073-1085). Innocent III (1198-1216) dealt with the nations of Europe as if they were his own fiefdoms.

In the third century, however, the Roman bishop was still a far cry from being the possessor of such power. To be sure, Victor I (189-198) had won a victory in the controversy concerning the Easter date. The synods which were convened at his initiative had spoken out against the practice of the church in Asia Minor. But by breaking off church fellowship with Asia Minor, Victor overshot the goal and thus incurred the disapproval of the churches in other areas. Besides, the Roman church itself was plagued by internal controversies and the role of the Roman bishops in these was not a happy one. The decisions of these bishops show clearly the naiveté of Rome when it came to theological questions. And finally, beneath the surface, a conflict was smouldering which was to split the Roman congregation into two camps. After the death of Zephyrinus, Victor's successor, the conflict erupted. Calixtus was elected bishop of Rome, no doubt by the majority. The minority, evidently made up of the influential and educated among the Roman Christians, chose Hippolytus as bishop. The congregation openly split into two parties, and pope and anti-pope fought bitterly with each other.

Hippolytus had this to say about his rival in his main work, *Refutation of All Heresies:* Calixtus had been the slave of a Christian who belonged to the imperial household. His master trusted him particularly because he was a Christian and transferred a large amount of money to him. Calixtus opened an exchange office and banking business with the entrusted monies, but went bankrupt. When exposure seemed imminent, he fled and reached the boat which he hoped would bring him to safety. Indeed, the boat's anchor was being weighed when Calixtus' master reached the scene. Calixtus threw himself into the sea but was saved from the waters by the sailors and turned over to his master, who committed him to the treadmill for punishment. Soon, however, he was released, for Calixtus asserted that there were debts outstanding which he could collect if he were free.

Evidently Calixtus' business transactions involved Jews, for one sabbath we find him involved in a disorder in the synagogue. In all probability he wanted only to make his debtors settle their accounts, but the Jews dragged him to court, charging him with violating their service. He was sentenced to the Sardinian mines. Here he found himself in the company of numerous other Christians who were condemned to death for the sake of their faith. Through the mediation of the imperial concubine, Marcia, who secretly was a Christian, these Christians were released. Calixtus was not among them. However, through entreaties and petitions he, too, was freed and appeared again in Rome. Hippolytus claims that Bishop Victor was horrified by this turn of events and, because of Calixtus' unsavory past, Victor immediately banished him from the city. However, after Victor's death, Calixtus succeeded in gaining greater and greater influence with Bishop Zephyrinus, until finally, after the bishop's death, he himself was elected bishop of Rome.

It is obvious from the above summary that what Hippolytus wrote about Calixtus was partly motivated by his hatred of the man. On the other hand, his report cannot be dismissed without further ado, for it contains a nucleus of truth. Yet Calixtus was elected bishop of Rome! Why? How? Had the Roman congregation lost its moral standards? No, it certainly knew what it was doing when it elected Calixtus, and not Hippolytus as bishop, and this action fits into a larger pattern. For at this election the question was not one of personalities but of essential differences.

Hippolytus was a scholar, and the congregation was dubious about his theological views, whereas Calixtus' understanding was much closer to that shared by the congregation as a whole. (Interestingly enough Rome's future theological development followed the line laid down by Hippolytus, and theological views similar to those of Calixtus soon became discredited and were condemned.) But without doubt Calixtus was the man the Roman congregation needed. He had an eye for the practical and a great skill in organizing, despite his earlier failure in the banking business. He hewed to the line of his predecessors whom he at least equalled in talents. (Even in Zephyrinus' time he exercised considerable influence over the church's affairs.)

Calixtus added decisively to the enhancement of the position of the Roman bishop by making him the judge over mortal sins. Formerly such sins were unforgivable, but now the bishop had the right to restore the sinner, after he had done public penance, to the fellowship of the church. There were three mortal sins: denial of God (apostasy from Christianity), murder, and unchastity. Murder was unthinkable for Christians. Since no persecution was threatening the congregation, there was no question concerning the sin of denying the faith. In effect, then, Calixtus' penitential edict referred almost exclusively to sins of unchastity. And such sins were not uncommon in a church which had increasingly more contact with the world—especially a church in a big city.

Of course, Hippolytus (and Tertullian as well) was critical of

Calixtus' treatment of moral offenses. But in the long run Calixtus was right. He did not want a church made up of the righteous only (as did Hippolytus and Tertullian), for that would have become a select church. He wanted a church which faced up to reality. The choice was between a church for saints only or a church that is a hospital for sinners. This was the issue at stake in the struggle between Calixtus and Hippolytus. The Roman congregation decided for Calixtus.

The split in the congregation lasted a long time. After the death of Calixtus a new bishop was elected by the majority party, and after his death another bishop, Pontianus, was elected. Hippolytus remained a rival bishop to both. In 235 a persecution against the Roman congregation broke out striking at both parties without distinction; pope and anti-pope were banished to Sardinia. This was the equivalent of a death sentence, and Pontianus and Hippolytus both died there. Pontianus, before being banished, had resigned his office so that a successor could be elected in Rome. Hippolytus, too, relinquished his claim to the bishop's office, thus making his peace with the Roman congregation. His body, along with that of Pontianus, was brought back home for solemn burial. Both were honored as martyrs.

Hippolytus was soon forgotten in Rome and in the West, chiefly because he wrote in Greek, which gave way to Latin as the language of the Roman church shortly after his death. Not until 1551 were the remains of the tombstone erected to his memory by the congregation found in the catacombs. On its base the titles of his works were listed. Much of his work is lost to us, but the most important writings have been preserved, although in some cases only fragments: we have his *Refutation of All Heresies,* his *Commentary on the Book of Daniel,* which was the first Christian exposition of the Bible as such, his *Chronicles,* his *Church Order,* and several others. Thanks to the devoted labor of many scholars, we have today, some seventeen hundred years after his death, a satisfactory picture of Hippolytus' personality and of his significance for theology and the church.

TERTULLIAN

A Passionate Theologian

All we know about Tertullian is based on incidental personal references and allusions that are scattered throughout his writings. Born in Carthage, he was the son of a Roman army officer. After completing his studies he practiced law in Rome, apparently with considerable success. A man with as much sagacity and dialectical skill as are displayed in his writings could hardly be anything but successful in the legal profession. He was a Gentile and probably led the kind of life in the big city that Augustine led during his youth. We do not know when he became a Christian or the date of his return to Carthage. In fact, we do not even know the year of his birth or of his death. All we can say with any degree of certainty is that he wrote between A.D. 195 and 220.

His first works were written after he had been a Christian for some time and was living in Carthage. We do not know what he did for a living at this time. In the opinion of some he was a presbyter (a pastor), according to others, a teacher of catechumens (those preparing for baptism). A third opinion is that he was simply a private citizen who had retired early and lived from the financial abundance accumulated in earlier years. This last theory is the least probable one, for such a long series of writings on theological subjects and questions facing the church could only have been written by someone who was more deeply involved in the service of the church than an average and private Christian would be. Furthermore, it is not likely that the church would have overlooked such a gifted and accomplished layman as Tertullian.

In any case, Tertullian was not a trained theologian. Nonetheless, he made such outstanding contributions to theology that the Western church drew upon them for centuries. Again and again the Roman popes used Tertullian's theological formulations in the doctrinal controversies which raged during the fourth and the fifth centuries. In the fourth century the Eastern church struggled mightily to work out a way of describing the relationship of Father and Son. The West had found a solution to this problem much earlier, for Tertullian had spoken of the "Trinity," in which Son and Holy Spirit are the second and third Persons of the Trinity whose members are "of one substance and one essence and one power." Following the Arian controversy, the East was torn by the so-called Christological controversies about the relationship of the divine to the human in Christ. The West had no need to undergo these controversies, for that which was finally crystallized in the East with difficulty had been developed by Tertullian and accepted in the West long before. Tertullian spoke of the fact that Christ is "God and man, one person in whom the two substances [divinity and humanity] are not mixed with each other but combined." Even though we cannot say that Tertullian was the only one who had thought this problem through and brought about a solution, his achievements were nonetheless outstanding. Moreover, it was Tertullian who taught the Latins to use their native tongue felicitously in the church. By coining a number of new words as well, he effected the conversion of pagan Latin into Christian Latin, the language of the Christian West.

Tertullian was a passionate man. In one of his writings, *Of Patience,* he admits that he does not possess too much of this virtue. But, he says, the sick speak best about health, so in this way he can speak of patience. When Tertullian took to the pen, the result was a polemic treatise. Another way of putting it is to say that Tertullian wrote to censure wrongs, repel attacks, and to refute false doctrines and teachers. And he did this with all the passion of his personality; he did not spare those who were the object of his attack, but he did not spare himself either.

For instance, when Tertullian wrote a treatise defending Christianity against the Gentiles, he began with the reproach that the Gentiles really know nothing of Christianity, yet they feel qualified to judge it. The accusations used against the Christians are unjust, he says. It is a violation of existing laws to attack Christians; if special laws are passed to permit such attacks, they are completely unjust. Thus, his introduction, the actual defense, is more of an attack. But then Tertullian really attacks: what the Gentiles reproach the Christians for—defection from the customs of the nation's forefathers, neglect of the gods, worship of animal deities, infanticide, incest, contempt for the imperial majesty—all this is found much more among the Gentiles themselves. Thus, Tertullian mocks, the Gentiles should shake hands with the Christians, for they themselves are guilty of all the crimes which they falsely impute to the Christians. He concludes with a relentless attack against the belief in pagan gods, which in every particular is proved as vain and unworthy of the deity.

In a work addressed to the provincial governors, Tertullian the lawyer attempted to appeal to the consciences of men who were charged with carrying out the persecution of Christians. And Tertullian boldly stood up against his own provincial governor when, on his own initiative, that official launched a persecution. Tertullian pointed out to him in a special writing what punishment had fallen on persecutors of Christians in the past and asked him if he was willing to risk this. Here as elsewhere we find—and this is a testimony of the self-assuredness of Tertullian and of the Christians of Africa—veiled threats: what would the governor do if the Christians of Carthage were to appear in a body before his residence? He asks in another place what would happen to the Roman Empire if the Christians would simply resort to passive resistance. Because of the large number of Christians, commerce and traffic would come to a halt and the empire would become unstable. Just go on persecuting the Christians, he calls triumphantly, instead of suppressing them; you only make them stronger. Blood is the seed which spreads Christianity.

Christianity is military service for the Lord, Tertullian tells Christians. Therefore, do not fear martyrdom; do not flee in persecution but face it courageously. Away with compromise! Do not listen to those who try to persuade you to make peace with the pagan system, to keep silent and not to irritate those in power. The Christian has nothing in common with them. Christians should withdraw from military service and public office, for they force a Christian, directly or indirectly, to serve paganism. Furthermore, a Christian should avoid observance of national holidays and celebrations and absent himself from the theater and public amusements, for they, too, are a part of pagan religion.

From what has been said thus far the reader can form a rather clear impression of what Tertullian was like. For him Christianity and the world have nothing in common. It is obvious that holding this conviction, Tertullian was bound to collide with the mainstream Catholic church, which by the beginning of the third century was beginning to conquer the world and to feel at home in the world. What the reaction of the official church was to Tertullian's many statements and writings on Christian customs and ethics is a matter of conjecture. In all probability his views on these subjects were not received with great enthusiasm. No doubt his ultimate break with the Catholic church was preceded by a period of growing estrangement and increasing conflict. When he finally realized the futility of trying to reconcile the path which the official church was following and the path which he considered to be the right one, Tertullian left the church and joined the movement called Montanism. Tertullian was not the only one to take this step; at that time a great many others also turned from the church to Montanism.

The years following Tertullian's defection to Montanism are a blank. There is a tradition that he eventually broke with Montanism. This is entirely possible in light of Tertullian's emotional makeup. But it is also possible that this legend was fostered by the mainstream church for its own purposes. His final years tarnished the reputation of Tertullian considerably, for he became carried away in vehemently attacking the church which he had once so brilliantly defended. Yet the very fact that his writings have been preserved so extensively indicates the value they had for the church which he ultimately renounced.

CYPRIAN

Outside the Church, No Salvation

The report about the Scillitan Martyrs in Numidia from the year 180 is the first information we have about Christianity in North Africa. Some time later we find in the writings of Tertullian news about Christians in other places in Africa; obviously there were not many. If Tertullian's list is complete, then Christianity still played a very modest role in Africa at the turn of the third century. Soon after, however, Christianity must have spread as if by storm. By the middle of the third century the Christian church in North Africa had two hundred and fifty bishops. The church did not grow in numbers only; it also gained an inner confidence and self-assurance. Furthermore, the North African church could boast of men whose use of the Latin tongue was outstanding. Among these were Tertullian (whose name, however, was scarcely mentioned, although the fruit of his labor was widely enjoyed), and Cyprian, who was bishop of Carthage, the capital, from 248 to 258.

It was nearly two hundred years before an African bishop (Augustine) exercised his office with an authority similar to that of Cyprian. One example of how Cyprian exerted his authority involved a letter written to him by the clergy of Rome. This letter criticized Cyprian's exercise of his office. He did not respond to the contents of the letter, but returned it with the message that the external appearance and the content made him doubt the genuineness of the letter. In addition to this he asked the Romans to investigate whether this truly was the letter they had written to him or whether it had been altered in transit. Another time there was an ecclesio-political entanglement (of which we shall speak directly) which involved the Roman bishop Cornelius. When Cornelius did not immediately act in the way that Cyprian had expected and considered correct, Cyprian wrote a letter in which he told Cornelius in plain language what he ought to do. And Cornelius acted accordingly!

The story of Cyprian's life reflects with particular clarity how things had changed in Africa. Thascius Caecilius Cyprianus came from a well-to-do and evidently noble family. By that time Christianity was no longer a religion of the lower classes but was gaining adherents from the upper classes and was able to choose its bishops from any stratum of society. Cyprian was born a Gentile shortly after 200. The circumstances of his family permitted him to receive a thorough education. But he became disenchanted with pleasure in the world about him, a world of luxury, vice, and moral turpitude. As time passed, his disenchantment and disgust deepened and Cyprian sought and obtained inner liberation by becoming a Christian. He himself relates how baptism opened the door to a new life for him. Now he dedicated all his strength to the service of the new faith, and in 248 or 249 the highest office of the church in his province was conferred on him.

He had held this post for scarcely a year when he was faced with difficult decisions as a result of the persecution unleashed by Emperor Decius. The persecution spread throughout Africa and concentrated on destroying the bishops, for a congregation without its leader was more easily scattered. Cyprian was faced with the question of what action should be taken under the circumstances. He decided to flee, or, more correctly speaking, to go into hiding. He left behind trusted men through whom he was kept in constant touch with what was going on. From his hideaway he regularly sent letters of advice and exhortations to the clergy who were leading the congregation during his enforced absence.

Cyprian was not the only bishop who chose this solution, which was not without risk, for all his possessions were left behind and subject to destruction or confiscation by the authorities. Nor was he acting against ecclesiastical regulations, although in his time Tertullian had adjured Christians not to evade persecution by flight. Nevertheless, Cyprian's decision to go into hiding was not everywhere understood. The Roman clergy, whose bishop, Fabian, had been the first to die a martyr's death during the persecution, wrote a critical letter (the one which Cyprian briskly sent back to Rome), and in Cyprian's own church his absence during this tumultuous time gave his opponents the long-sought opportunity to carry out intrigues against him. This caused severe discord in the African church of which we will have to speak in still greater detail in another section. There is no question but that Cyprian, if he had had to make his decision over again, would have decided differently. For the rest of his life he had to struggle with the difficulties which arose from his absence in this time of persecution.

Shortly after his return, when the persecution was still continuing although its initial fury was spent, he began his efforts to reassume control of his church. He was successful, for not only did he have the law on his side, his personal qualities were far superior to those of his opponents. The various synods as well as the Roman church accepted his point of view regarding those who had lapsed from Christianity during the persecution. Cyprian expounded his position thoroughly in a special treatise *On the Lapsed*. In this writing he advocated not a gentle wrist slapping, but a just punishment for those who had frivolously denied Christianity. If they wanted to return to the church, they had to do so as penitents. Only those who had weakened as a result of torture could expect a shortened period of penitence. Two years after Cyprian's return there were indications of a new persecution. This made it possible to restore to the followship of the church those penitents who had proved in the meantime their serious desire to return.

With that, the difficult controversies were brought to a happy conclusion. Cyprian had asserted himself and strengthened the bishop's position. But the split in the African church remained, and when the splinter church started to crumble (thanks largely to Cyprian), the return of its adherents to the Catholic church caused a new and bitter controversy, this time between the African and the Italian churches. This controversy raged about the validity of the baptism administered by the rival church. Did those whom that church had baptized have to be rebaptized? For Cyprian the matter was clear: outside of the church there is no salvation. He who does not have the church for a mother, cannot have God for a father. He had said this before, during the controversy about the lapsed in Carthage. How can there be sacraments outside the Catholic church? How can a baptism be valid if it is not performed by the Catholic church? The upshot was that those baptized by the rival church had to be baptized a second time.

Opposition arose, and it came from Rome. In Rome Pope Stephen I had succeeded Cornelius, and he was made of sterner stuff. He wrote with insulting sharpness and argued that since the rival church had given recognition to Catholic baptism, the Catholic church would be well advised to recognize the baptism of its former rival. This did not deter Cyprian, who did not even think of giving up his point of view. At a specially convened synod the African bishops present came forward, one after the other, agreeing with Cyprian in explicit statements. The result was a break between the churches. Once before a Roman bishop had broken off fellowship with another church province— Pope Victor I in the Easter controversy with Asia Minor. Now Stephen I took the same measures toward Africa. This was an indication that Rome's claim to supremacy in the church was continuing to grow stronger. However, the passionate objections of Cyprian and the other bishops show that this claim to supremacy was premature—the other churches had no intention of submitting. The controversy was resolved only after the death of Stephen, and even then it was a difficult task.

Those were the last years of Cyprian. The persecution of the Christians under Emperor Valerian brought him to his fulfillment. Having been banished from his home city of Carthage, he was permitted to return once more. But he knew that the time granted him would be brief. Once again, when arrest and deportation were imminent, he took to flight, not in order to avoid persecution, but in order not to die outside of Carthage. He achieved what he intended. In a suburb of Carthage, his head fell under the executioner's axe on September 14, 258. A report of his death has been preserved which testifies to the love and respect of his congregation, which had gathered at the place of his arrest and execution. "We want to be beheaded with him" was their cry to the tribunal which had condemned him. The report also testifies to the dignity displayed by Cyprian at the hearing before the governor and in his death.

The fame of Cyprian shone supreme until Augustine's put it in the shade. Up to then Cyprian was *the* theological writer of the Latin-speaking church, despite his position on the question of baptism, which differed from the later ecclesiastical attitude and which Augustine attempted to justify with great effort. Yet his treatises are not his most significant contribution, for in them he is strongly dependent on Tertullian. He was a man without personal ambition; he took up the pen only when urgent necessities demanded it. His personality is reflected with more intensity in his letters, where he appears as the great leader of his church. He had no equal in the church of the West, not only in his own time, but for years to come.

NOVATUS AND NOVATIAN

Personal Ambition

Internal discord in the churches of Carthage and Rome! This is the picture conjured up before our eyes by the names of two men, Novatus and Novatian. They were as different as two men can be, and yet as allies the two had a devastating effect.

The background for the events in Rome and Carthage lies in the edict issued by Emperor Decius for the whole Roman Empire toward the end of 249, a few years after his accession to the throne. At first the edict seemed to be relatively harmless: all citizens of the empire were to be examined about their attitude toward the deities that sustained the empire. Furthermore, citizens were to prove their loyalty to the gods by performing an act of sacrifice. In effect, however, this edict called for a most extensive persecution of the Christians.

The empire was in danger; therefore, all its strength had to be mustered for survival. That was the watchword of the day. Anyone who refused to sacrifice was regarded as a Christian. On the other hand, if he participated in the sacrifice only for fear of losing his job, having his property confiscated, or being imprisoned and martyred, and wanted to remain a Christian in his heart, he was separated from the church. The way back to the fold was very difficult, for the church considered every one who participated in the sacrifice an apostate, even if that person regarded the act of sacrifice as nothing more than an external ceremony.

The opinion of the Roman authorities was that once a person became separated from the fellowship of the church, he would drift back to paganism, and that anyone who held to the faith despite persuasion and other blandishments, would have to be imprisoned or executed. Holding these principles, the commissions started to work throughout the empire. And it seemed they calculated correctly, for everywhere the number of defectors was large. Even some of the bishops renounced their faith. The church had lived in peace for too long. Persecutions which had flared up from time to time had been limited to individual cities or territories. Now for the first time the angel of death swept through the whole empire and found the church unprepared.

In Rome Bishop Fabian was one of the first to fall victim to the persecution. The Roman Christians did not dare to elect a successor, for that would have meant condemning the new bishop to immediate martyrdom, so for a while the congregation was led by all the clergy in common. The leading writer among them was the presbyter Novatian, a man proven in every respect and distinguished by his theological learning. Several of his writings show that he was a significant theological thinker and a proficient churchman. Thus he had reason to expect that he would be elected to the bishop's office. But when the persecution finally abated and the time for the election came, not he, but the presbyter Cornelius was chosen by an overwhelming majority. Novatian's ambition was thwarted, and he was deeply offended. Along with five of his friends he refused to consent to the election of Cornelius. This did not change the result, but it indicated that a repetition of what had happened during the time of Hippolytus was threatening.

It did not take long until Novatian was elected counter-bishop. Where there is a will there is a way, and in the history of the church it seems that that way takes the following direction: one designs as attractive a program as possible and then woos adherents to it. Naturally, it is not because someone wants to satisfy his offended personal ambition or because he strives for power! The reason usually given is that someone has gained new theological insights and wants to put them into effect, or better still, has to put them into effect. The danger inherent in this is obvious, but this is the way it has always been done, and this is the way Novatian did it also.

Novatian did not have to look long for a program; it almost offered itself. The urgent question of his time was how to treat those who had defected from the church during the persecution—the lapsed, as they were called. As soon as the persecution abated, they streamed back to the church. Bishop Cornelius was inclined toward clemency, but Novatian rallied those who opposed the reception of the lapsed. Actually, during the vacancy in the bishop's office, he had taken the same position as Cornelius now took. But reversing his stand, he now advocated a severity similar to that of the ancient church. And since many in the church were of the same opinion, his party increased rapidly. He was expelled from the church by a synod convened by Cornelius, but that was immaterial. His expulsion was received as a crown of martyrdom imposed on one unjustly persecuted by the official church. Anyway, Rome was only one city, not the whole world. He turned successfully to Antioch and to other dioceses. Innocence was being persecuted, who would not want to come to its aid? In Antioch and elsewhere only Novatian's persecuted innocence, not his real motive, was seen. If the bishop of Antioch had not died just at that time, a great synod of the East probably would have endorsed the principles of Novatian.

That Novatian was driven by ambition and not by genuine responsibility is shown, in addition to his change of position, by his alliance with the lapsed of Carthage. There the bishop was in favor of a strict attitude toward the lapsed, whereas his opponents were in favor of leniency. But there was also a group who were dissatisfied with their bishop. Some presbyters had looked upon the election of Cyprian as bishop of Carthage with displeasure. They were led by a man named Novatus. At first they had no lever to use against Cyprian. But the new bishop, inexperienced in his office, was bound to show a weak spot. When

Cyprian, in the first year of the persecution by Decius, went into hiding and was separated from his congregation, the desired opportunity to undermine the authority of the bishop presented itself. He could not openly be attacked for fleeing, but his enemies could make use of the disputes which arose in Carthage in regard to the treatment of the lapsed.

The "Confessors," those who had endured the threats and tortures of the persecution without defecting from the faith and who had managed to survive (by no means were all confessors executed), demanded the recognition of their standing right to determine whether leniency should be shown toward the lapsed. If they issued a "letter of peace," a certificate of discharge, to one who had defected in the persecution, the church would have to receive that person back into its fellowship without further ado and without penitential punishment. What the confessors claimed was that by virtue of their steadfast holding to the faith, the spirit of Christ had come upon them in their sufferings. And if a confessor pardoned one who had lapsed, then it was as if Christ himself had done it.

Cyprian, still absent from Carthage, would not bow to the claim advanced by the confessors. Theory and practice were far from identical with them. The certificates of discharge were often given out lightly by the confessors, without close examination of those who desired them. Some confessors even gave such letters in the form of blank endorsements. The name was left out, and thus the door to abuse was open. It was even possible to receive letters of peace for payment. Furthermore, the lives of many of the confessors were at times anything but blameless. As long as the persecution lasted, Cyprian opposed any decision in the question of the restitution of the lapsed. If anyone wanted to repent of his apostasy, there was ample opportunity to do so; all such a penitent had to do was to go before the civil authorities and revoke his act of sacrifice. Martyrdom, which was bound to follow such an act, would purge him from his former lapse and make him again a fully accepted member of the church.

The confessors were not inclined to go along with Cyprian's views. They declared that he disregarded their honorary rights, and they were not alone in this. The presbyters opposing Cyprian strengthened their position by receiving back into church fellowship all who presented letters of peace and admitting them to Holy Communion. Thus the confessors pushed their claims higher and higher until they finally issued a general amnesty for all the lapsed and demanded that Cyprian accept their action as valid.

With this demand the confessors definitely put themselves in the wrong, but Novatus and his adherents did not object at all. One of the confessors became the administrator of the ecclesiastical aid fund. Only those who allied themselves with the cause of the confessors and Novatus against Cyprian could receive financial assistance from the fund. When Cyprian finally returned to Carthage (the first wave of persecution was past, but it had by no means ended) he found the congregation in open rebellion. As was to be expected, the synodical conventions confirmed his position, but this did not impress his opponents, since they were interested only in power and not in justice or the church. Indeed, they said that they acted in the interest of the church, but if they had really done so, they would have endangered the further existence of their own party. They then elected a counter-bishop and entered into a relationship with Novatian, even though he was an advocate of the exactly opposite view. Federation with him, however, brought reinforcements to their own position and was able to make the situation still more difficult for Cyprian. Novatus and his party engaged in propaganda for recognition in Rome, and if Cyprian had been less energetic and had not influenced the Roman bishop Cornelius, the Roman church might have recognized them. Similarly Novatian tried for recognition in Carthage, but even with Novatus' help he was unsuccessful.

We do not hear what significance the party of Novatus had in the long run. In his letters, Cyprian always dismissed his opponents with very few words, as though they were of little account. However, the counter-church organized by Novatian flourished for centuries afterward in various places. And in regard to the question of those who turned back from Novatian to the Catholic church, a serious dispute arose between Africa and Rome, as we have seen. It is in such ways that the ambition of individuals can endanger the church.

DIONYSIUS OF ALEXANDRIA

How Is Jesus God?

In July, 260, after the great persecution had ended, the presbyter Dionysius was elected bishop of Rome. In Alexandria the bishop was also a man named Dionysius. Thus two men of the same name stood at the head of the two most important Christian communities. The Alexandrian was without doubt the more important of the two men. When we read fragments of his writings we have to agree that he was rightly called "the Great." He had also held the bishop's post longer than his Roman counterpart. His election as bishop had taken place several years before the persecution launched by Emperor Decius and he had steered his church successfully and prudently through the time of oppression. He had taken an active role in such internal church conflicts as the struggle between Cornelius and Novatian and in the disputes over baptism administered by those who had left the church to form a rival fellowship. In each case he acted in a way that meets with our approval. He opposed the claims of Novatian and supported the authority of Cornelius. On the other hand, he alleviated as much as possible the harshness with which Roman Bishop Stephen dealt with all who disagreed with him on the baptism question. A split in the Roman church was averted, thanks largely to Dionysius of Alexandria.

Despite this he was defeated in the dispute with Dionysius of Rome. Theologically, the Alexandrian was a disciple of Origen, as were the majority of Eastern theologians. Even if they rejected the person of Origen and found fault with his theological system in this or that point, they could not go back to an earlier theological position and so they were forced to use Origen's way of thinking and expression. Things were different in the West, however, where Origen was virtually unknown. There the influence of the earlier Tertullian was dominant. It is true that Tertullian had been banned because of his defection to Montanism and that he was officially proscribed. But the same thing happened in the West with respect to Tertullian as had happened in the East with respect to Origen: the church simply could not avoid his theological formulations. Often the church used his formulations unconsciously in its theology, little realizing that it was dependent on a schismatic. So for all practical purposes the dispute between Dionysius of Alexandria and Dionysius of Rome was a dispute between the thought of Origen and Tertullian, although, to be precise, we must say that Tertullian was only superficially understood.

The point at issue in the dispute was the question of Jesus' sonship. Two things have been fundamental for Christianity through the ages: (1) that in Christ God came to earth, and (2) that there is only one God. The problem was how to reconcile these two statements. This was not a problem for the earliest Christians—the two statements were taught and accepted simultaneously without any difficulty. Without any embarrassment Ignatius of Antioch could speak of God suffering on the cross. Controversy with those groups that differed from the mainstream church, as well as the internal development of the church, forced Christians to think more deeply about how the divinity of Jesus could be combined with the fact of the one God who revealed himself to the world as the creator and as the father of Jesus Christ. This thinking led to difficulties and disputes.

By the end of the second century two solutions seemed to have been found. One solution started with the historical Jesus, with the man who walked in Palestine. According to this view the power of God descended on him at his baptism in the Jordan

River and took up habitation in him. From this point on, Jesus was enabled to perform divine deeds; before that he was different from other people because of special purity and righteousness, but otherwise he was a man like all others. The second solution declared that the Jesus Christ of the Gospels was a mode or form of God's presence. God is active in three modes: Creator, Son, and Holy Spirit. But it is always the same Father God who reveals himself to man, only in different ways. This solution, it was thought, made it possible to maintain the unity of God against pagan polytheism while at the same time doing justice to the Scriptures. Because of the stress on the unity of God, the theologians who advocated these two solutions came to be known as Monarchians. They played a role first in Asia Minor and then in Rome. Their teaching found wide acceptance and many adherents, particularly among the laity.

The theology of the church advanced beyond this stage of thinking only after long, involved disputes. Very soon theologians recognized that the solution offered by Monarchianism was only a pseudo-solution. The first solution (called dynamistic Monarchianism), advocated by Theodotius and others, assumed that Jesus was a man who was changed at baptism by the power of God. But if this were the case, the problem was that Christ had his beginning in time, and therefore his divinity is somewhat short of full divinity. If it is assumed with so-called modalistic Monarchianism, advocated by Noetius, Sabellius and others, that Christ was only a form of appearance of the deity, then we cannot speak of a Holy Trinity and we are led by necessity to the statement that at Golgotha it was God the Father who was nailed to the cross.

The Apologists, Tertullian, Hippolytus, and especially Origen were the theologians who overcame Monarchianism. In their thinking, Christ is eternally with the Father, as the beginning of John's Gospel states. He is with God from eternity, yet he is distinct from him. This theological statement was much less easily understood than that of Monarchianism, and the result was that this new direction in theology, the so-called logos-theology, had a difficult time in setting forth its insights and getting a hearing. (The term logos-theology derived from John 1:1, where the Greek word *logos* ["word"] was used.) The Roman bishops adopted this theology around the turn of the third century, but this move was not made without great difficulty. Even after Monarchianism had been rejected officially, logos-theologians were for a long time able to make only awkward statements about the relationship of Jesus Christ to the Father. If it had not been for Tertullian, who had coined completely clear formulas or ways of expressing this relationship, the theologians would have been helpless. At least by using his terms they could approximate a description of the relationship. One suspects, however, that they did not always understand the matter. This situation did not change until the fourth century when the dispute reached its peak in the Arian controversy.

Nevertheless, as already mentioned, the Roman bishop Dionysius was victorious over his Egyptian namesake in the dispute concerning the position of Jesus Christ within the Trinity. It happened in this way. In Egypt quite a few Christians embraced the old Monarchian thought forms and distrusted the statements of the theologians influenced by Origen. Dionysius of Alexandria had pointed out to them emphatically that Father and Son could not be seen as a unity, as the Monarchians held. But in the heat of battle he shot far beyond his immediate objectives. He went so far as to state that Christ is as different from God as is the vine from the gardener who takes care of it, or the boat from the carpenter who built it. Word of his theological aberration reached Rome, and he was officially called to task by his Roman colleague. Although the Roman bishop did not have anything essential to contribute to the matter at issue itself, he succeeded in persuading the Alexandrian that his formulations had gone too far, and he withdrew them, but without abandoning his basic position.

The retraction by Dionysius no doubt satisfied his Egyptian opponents as well as the Roman bishop. But such a compromise did not settle the problem. Fifty years later the struggle flared up anew.

This time discussion of the problem of Jesus' sonship was not limited to Egypt but involved the whole church of the East. When that happened Rome was not able to end the dispute with a letter from its bishop. A great many synods were convened at which the matter was reviewed and discussed again and again. It was Arius who made possible the final resolution of the question by triggering a dispute known as the Arian controversy.

DIOCLETIAN

Persecution Fails

The persecution inaugurated by Emperor Decius was a planned attempt by paganism to suppress Christianity, which by the third century had increased greatly both in influence and in magnitude. How many Christians were executed or imprisoned it is impossible to say. Certainly the number was considerable. But there were a great many Christians, including bishops, who did not persevere in their faith during the persecution. The bishop of Smyrna sacrificed to the gods and solemnly renounced Christianity. Two bishops in Spain turned over the holy writings of the churches to the persecutors, an act which was tantamount to apostasy. Especially vulnerable to the persecution were Christians of means, for all their possessions were subject to confiscation if they refused to deny their faith. Yet the authorities made it so easy to retain one's possessions! A few bits of incense strewn into the sacrificial flame, and one was safe. But this act was an explicit denial of Christ.

Of course, it was also possible to buy one's way out of the persecution. All one had to do was to pay a bribe to a corrupt official, and he would be willing to issue a certificate to the effect that a sacrifice had been made, when in fact it had not. But Christians who purchased such certificates were also regarded as having denied Christ. It is truly astonishing that the number of the lapsed was not larger than some sources have reported. Perhaps these sources even exaggerate, for what Christian preacher of repentance in any age does not paint the situation blackest of black?

Even if the number of the martyrs and of the lapsed was as large as reports would lead us to believe, the subsequent course of history shows that the persecution of Decius did not achieve its goal; it spent its fury within one year. The number of the steadfast was too large, and the power of the state just was not great enough to force the Christians back to paganism. The officials became weary, and when Emperor Decius fell shortly afterward in battle agâinst the Goths, the persecution ceased altogether. From time to time in later years the attempt was made to renew the persecution. Emperors Gallus and Valerian issued decrees similar to that of Decius, but the danger was past. When Gallienus became sole ruler in 260, he revoked all the edicts which had dealt with the persecution of the Christians and even issued regulations not to annoy them. Christianity emerged victorious over its persecutors.

Of course, local persecutions broke out from time to time, but in general the church was left in peace and was able to commence repairing the damage done by the persecutions. The interval of peace lasted forty years, and during those years the strength of the church grew mightily. New converts streamed to the church in greater numbers from all levels of society. Christians were to be found in all classes and among the highest officials of the state; they were even at the imperial court. The number of Christians serving in the army increased steadily. At the same time the state began to respect the Christian faith of its officials. In the course of an altercation in the church of Antioch, for example, the contesting parties appealed to the emperor, and his decision was rendered as impartially as if the Christian church had been an officially recognized institution.

Thus one might think that it was only a question of time until Christianity would be given equal rights with the various pagan religions of the empire. But this was not the case. Christianity did not achieve recognition until paganism had once more arisen to do desperate and bloody battle against the church, and Christian blood had flowed in great streams.

This persecution is linked with the name of Emperor Diocletian, the soldier-emperor who rose from the ranks of the army and who put the Roman Empire on a new foundation. He probably was not the true instigator of the persecution; more likely it was his co-emperor, Galerius, who was the precipitator. Diocletian himself was too prudent a tactician to instigate a persecution of the Christians, especially since Christianity had penetrated his own family (his wife and his daughter were sympathetic to Christianity, if not baptized Christians). But Galerius knew how to arouse Diocletian to the point at which, overwhelmed with anger, he would let his passion have free reign.

Galerius played on Diocletian's superstition. It was customary to predict the future by reading the entrails of sacrificed animals. Because of their position, the Christian court officials also had to be present at such readings. On one such occasion, when the priests did not find an answer, the failure was blamed on the presence of the Christians, who made the sign of the cross to protect themselves against the demons. It was said that it was the Christians' fault that the voice of the gods was silent. All court officials were then commanded to perform the sacrifice. Those who refused were to be scourged. At the same time the order was issued to purge the army of Christians. Diocletian wanted to leave it at that, but Galerius urged him on. The emperor's military and legal advisers were in favor of a general suppression of the Christian church because it had become too powerful. Then Diocletian, who was rooted completely in the old faith, gave in. Lactantius reports the progress of events in a vivid manner.

At dawn a troop of loyal soldiers moved toward the church of Nicomedia, which was located near the palace. The doors were broken in, the church was plundered, the Scriptures found in it burned. Diocletian and Galerius watched the spectacle from the tower of the palace. At first the church was supposed to be burned, but the emperors were afraid the fire might ignite the whole city, so instead military engineers levelled the house of God. The following day an edict was posted declaring that the Christians had forfeited their civil rights. An approaching Christian who tore the edict down became the first victim; he was cruelly put to death. But the persecution was kept within bounds. Galerius wanted to encourage further persecution, so he had the imperial palace put to the torch and had the blame thrown on the Christians. Surely only Christians could be the perpetrators of such a dastardly deed. It was common knowledge that they were enemies of the state, and now, because of the edict against them, revenge had driven them to attack the person of the emperor himself. Now the wrath of Diocletian flared up. He himself sat in judgment and attempted to find by torture who among his entourage was secretly in league with the Christians. Naturally the investigation was without result, for the entourage of Galerius, among whom the arsonists were to be found, remained unmolested. Although it is uncertain whether Lactantius' assertion that Galerius himself was responsible for starting the fire is true, it is possible, for it would not be the first or last time that arson would be used to arouse passions, remove undesirable elements, and achieve political goals.

Two weeks later Galerius repeated the successful maneuver with still better results. The investigations of Diocletian went further afield, and his distrust grew steadily. Not only the imperial entourage but also the higher officials were forced to sacrifice, and if they refused, they were cruelly put to death. Diocletian's suspicions extended even to his wife and daughter. Gradually he convinced himself of the existence of a full-scale Christian conspiracy. In Antioch a rebellion which probably had nothing at all to do with Christianity was suppressed with unusual severity. A command was issued to imprison all clergy and to force them to make the required sacrifice. Finally, sacrifice was demanded from every Christian in the empire, as it had been in the time of Emperor Decius. Soon enraged passions began to flare up and were surreptitiously encouraged both by Galerius and the emperor of the West, Maximianus.

It is horrifying to read the reports of what happened. Incense was actually strewn into the sacrificial flame from the hands of men and women who had lost consciousness from the pain of torture. This was the only way the required sacrifice could be obtained; the resistance of Christians could not be broken in any other way. In Africa a whole congregation of forty-nine Christians was arrested at a forbidden celebration of the Lord's Supper and summarily executed. In Asia Minor a whole town with all of its Christian inhabitants was burned to the ground. Punishments were so severe that the gouging of an eye or the crippling of a leg was looked upon as leniency. Those thus crippled were sent into the mines as slave laborers. But even in the mines they continued to keep their faith and to celebrate their services as if nothing had happened!

That was the persecution of Diocletian. Perhaps the persecution should bear the names of Galerius and Maximinus Daja instead, for Diocletian was responsible only for the first two years. In A.D. 305 he abdicated and went into retirement, and the persecution was carried on by Galerius and Maximinus Daja. The other emperors or coregents who were in power at that time also participated actively in the persecution. (Under Diocletian there was a very complex system of coemperors and regents.) To the best of our knowledge there were only two rulers who did not share the hostility of their colleagues against the Christians: Constantius (the father of Constantine), who reigned in Gaul, and Maxentius, in Italy.

Finally, in the year 311 the persecution had run its full course. Shortly before his death Galerius issued an edict of toleration in which he confessed the failure of his attempt to wipe out Christianity and ordered the persecution stopped. But in the next year a means of circumventing this order was found. The pagan city magistrates were requested to direct petitions to the new ruler asking him to expel the Christians from their cities. Such petitions were gladly granted and the petitioners were rewarded so generously that no doubt remained about the attitude toward Christians on the part of the highest authority. As a result the number of such petitions increased steadily. It can be said that paganism left no stone unturned in blocking Christianity's way to victory. But it was all in vain. While the successors of Diocletian cast about for a new way of eliminating Christianity, a complete turn of events was quietly underway. One year after the death of Diocletian a young man named Constantine fled from the court of Galerius to his father, Constantius, in Gaul. And with that a new epoch began.

CONSTANTINE

A Decisive Supporter

In the preceding section it was stated that the persecution of Diocletian could also bear the name of Galerius. In reality it was Galerius who was the evil genius behind the persecution, the one man who both prolonged and intensified it. The motives that moved Galerius, just a few days before his death, on April 30, A.D. 311, to order the cessation of the persecution must have been powerful ones. Was remorse in the hour of his death for innocent blood one of them? Probably not; he was not the kind of man to feel remorse. Was it the realization that his efforts to stamp out Christianity had been futile? Perhaps! But that alone would not have been sufficient. Something else must have been behind his action. That other factor was the influence of Constantine, whom we mentioned at the end of the last section.

The text of Galerius' edict shows how reluctant he really was to stop the persecution. "For the prosperity and welfare of the republic," it says at the beginning, he had tried, in "harmony with the ancient laws and public order," to take care that the Christians "who had left the religion of their fathers should come back to reason; since, indeed, the Christians themselves, for some reason, had followed such a caprice and had fallen into such a folly that they . . . at their own will and pleasure . . . would thus make laws unto themselves which they should observe." But despite all efforts "most of them persevered in their determination. . . . In view of our most mild clemency and the constant habit by which we are accustomed to grant indulgence to all," he would like to permit the Christians now, "that they may again be Christians . . . provided they do nothing contrary to good order." More detailed directions, the edict continued, would be issued to officials of the imperial court.

Two years later, in January, 313, Constantine, who had become emperor of the West along with Licinius, issued a similar edict, the Edict of Milan. This document has a ring quite different from that of Galerius' edict. Repeatedly it states that all regulations concerning the Christians until now (that is, the edicts of persecution) are, without exception, invalidated, and that the Christians are permitted "to observe the Christian religion . . . freely and openly." Further: all church buildings and other church property which had been confiscated was to be returned to the Christians without delay, even if such property had, in the meantime, come into the hands of others. Present owners of confiscated Christian property were to be compensated by the public treasury. This edict was to be promulgated everywhere by public announcement so that all should know the desire of the rulers.

This really meant freedom. In the tenth book of his *Church History*, Eusebius, who lived through this period, expressed the jubilation of the Christians of that time: "O sing unto the Lord a new song; for he hath done marvelous things. . . . After those terrible and gloomy spectacles and narratives, we were accounted worthy now to behold and to celebrate in panegyric such things as of a truth many righteous men and martyrs of God before us desired to see upon earth and saw them not, and to hear, and heard them not. . . . So the whole human race was freed from the oppression of the tyrants. And, delivered from his former ills, each one after his own fashion acknowledged as the only true God Him who was the Champion of the pious. But we especially, who had fixed our hopes upon the Christ of God, had gladness unspeakable."

The tide had turned! Christianity had achieved freedom. It stood now with equal legal rights, side by side with the other religions and cults. Not that Christianity had become the recognized state religion, as many think; but at least the state was no longer against the church. The church now had the opportunity to compete peacefully and legally with paganism for the souls of men. In the opinion of the Christians there could be no doubt what the result of this competition would be. Paganism, which was gradually crumbling, could not permanently resist a faith which had withstood all the attacks and persecutions of a hostile empire.

This turn of events was due to the great Emperor Constantine. Certainly, the coemperor Maxentius also was friendly toward Christianity, but his benevolent government applied only in a part of the empire and would not have changed the total situation of the church. In the East the spirit of persecution was still rampant. Even Constantine's brother-in-law and original ally, Licinius, began to suppress the Christians when he became the sole ruler in the East. Only the victory of Constantine over all contenders for power in the empire guaranteed the Christians observance of the Edict of Milan and true freedom.

Constantine had come to power within a relatively short time. In 306 he had fled from Rome to his father Constantius Chlorus of Gaul. Just a few months later his father died and Constantine was immediately proclaimed as successor by the military. This meant that Constantine was ruler of Gaul and Britain. Up to the year 311 he was occupied with consolidating and strengthening his own position in his own realm. The German tribes on the border of the Rhine gave him a great deal of trouble, but Constantine's bold military expeditions subdued them. The battles with Germans sharpened the fighting ability of Constantine's troops and gave him valuable field experience as a commander in chief. These two factors were of decisive importance when Galerius died on May 5, 311. The time had come for a new alignment of power.

Constantine let the East fight out its own controversies and turned his attention to seizing sole rule in the West. In a completely unexpected and rapid maneuver he marched over the Alps, through Italy, to Rome. On October 28, 312, at the Milvian Bridge before the walls of the city, the decisive battle between Maxentius and him took place. Maxentius' army was routed, and in fleeing over a wooden bridge that had been erected over the Tiber he fell into the river and drowned. With that, Rome, and at the same time Italy, Africa, and Spain were under the control of Constantine. A year later Licinius succeeded in obtaining complete control of the East. Now there were only two rulers instead of the numerous rivals for power of just a few years before. Soon there was a showdown between these two, first in 314, and finally in 324. Licinius was defeated and the rule of the world lay in the hands of one man. Thus Constantine seemed to restore the era of strong emperors which had characterized the second and third centuries.

There was one difference, however, which was very significant for the future: this emperor, Constantine, was a Christian. To be sure, he was not a Christian in the sense that he would have successfully passed an examination in theology. Nor was he a Christian in the sense that the influence of Christianity could be visibly discerned in the internal affairs of the empire and in the attitude of the emperor. That was not to be expected, for throughout the empire, pagans were still by far in the majority, especially among the officials, in the nobility, and in the army. Even in Asia Minor where the Christians were most concentrated, they scarcely numbered half the population. In all other provinces the percentage of Christians was often much less. Furthermore, the empire had been rooted for centuries in the old pagan traditions; these could not be broken and abolished overnight. Carefully planned action was required.

Constantine's cautiousness has not always been understood, and therefore too often he is portrayed even by prominent scholars, as one who was not a Christian at all. We are told that he only pretended to be a Christian for the sake of expediency. Why would it be expedient to be a Christian since the empire was predominantly pagan? Certainly many deeds in the life of Constantine cannot be defended, but without doubt he wanted to be a Christian. The Christian faith Constantine confessed at his death was probably his from earliest youth. As far as he was concerned, he had bidden leave to the old gods; he helped Christianity to victory in the world. He performed tremendous deeds as a soldier and as a statesman. The political system developed by him has long since disappeared; very few people today remember that such a system ever existed. One thing people do remember: Constantine gave his protection and his support to the Christian church at a decisive moment in history.

DONATUS

Defeat out of Victory

After a struggle that lasted for several centuries, the church finally achieved equality with the other religions of the Roman Empire. Tremendous sacrifices had been made: thousands upon thousands had suffered and many had died for their faith. Now the battle was over. The state had seen that it could not suppress Christianity. The new ruler was ready to further the church, and the door that led to supremacy was opened. And in the long run no religion could resist Christianity, which had defeated all other cults despite terrible oppression.

At this time, when the dream of centuries was fulfilled, the church was disunited internally. It is really lamentable that at the very moment external pressure was removed, the church was splintered by bitter controversies. In the West, especially in Africa, it was the Donatist controversy; in the East, it was first the Arian and then the Christological controversy which dissipated the energies of the church. And the worst of it is that these controversies were largely power struggles. The Donatists in any case were clearly concerned with gaining power in the church. Their first interest was success, and they cared very little about the means employed. Naturally ecclesiastical and theological differences also played a role, but they were of secondary significance. The Arian and the so-called Christological controversies were different matters. Here theological questions were in the forefront, and the issue was one of religious differences. But here, too, the matter of ecclesiastical power and church politics combined until this controversy also degenerated into a pure power struggle. But we will speak of this later. Here we are concerned with Donatism.

The controversy began with Constantine's accession to the throne. One of the emperor's first acts was to direct the proconsul of Africa to restore to the Christian church all the possessions which had been confiscated during the Diocletian persecution. In addition, the emperor had established a fund from which grants were to be distributed to deserving clergymen by the bishop of the North African church. But which churches were to receive the possessions and which bishop was to administer the fund? The emperor and the magistrates soon found out to their astonishment that there were two bishops and two Christian groups in North Africa, each of which vigorously denied that the other was Christian.

How had that come about? We have to go back to the time of the Diocletian persecution to give even a partial explanation of this state of affairs. At that time Mensurius was bishop of Carthage, and the archdeacon Caecilian was his right-hand man. The congregation and the bishopric appeared to be divided into several camps. The question of how one should act in persecution was a burning issue which in North Africa reached all the way back to the controversies of Montanus against Tertullian and Novatus against Cyprian. But other factors, very human factors, also played a significant role. For example, there was a wealthy lady in Carthage by the name of Lucilla. It was her custom, before receiving Holy Communion, to kiss the relic of a martyr which she carried with her. Caecilian publicly reprimanded her for this superstitious act, and in so doing he offended her deeply. She never forgave him and wanted to avenge herself. During the lifetime of Bishop Mensurius, therefore, Lucilla's home was a gathering place for those who were dissatisfied with the official church and its leaders.

When Bishop Mensurius died (a few years before the accession of Constantine) and Caecilian was chosen as his successor, the opposition took action. They elected a counter-bishop, Maiorinus,

Lucilla's personal chaplain, a fact which makes the background of the events relatively clear. Lucilla now took full revenge on Caecilian. Her money probably played a very important role, enabling her to acquire a considerable following. But other factors also played a role. One of these factors was regional differences, for it was the Numidian bishops who elected Maiorinus as successor of Mensurius, evidently because they had not been consulted in the election of Caecilian. Another factor was the feeling that during the persecution Mensurius and Caecilian had not acted as many thought they should have acted.

But how could the election of Caecilian, an accomplished fact, be invalidated? The only way that the election of Maiorinus could be justified according to church law was to assert that Caecilian's consecration was invalid because he had been consecrated by traditors, that is, bishops who during the persecution had surrendered the Scriptures to the authorities. Under such circumstances Caecilian's consecrators would not be legitimate consecrators of a bishop. Here a theological contrast can be seen, the only one of which one can speak at all, the belief that the effectiveness of an ecclesiastical action is dependent upon the purity of the person who performs it. This is understandable since a clergyman is supposed to have the attributes of purity and holiness. But can the validity of an ecclesiastical act be based on the purity of an individual? Should a baptism be valid only if the minister who performs it is a holy man? That would make men the standard and would degrade the sacrament itself. After all, the promise of the Lord is given to a child not because the pastor who baptizes him is an exemplary man, but because the Lord commanded that the child be baptized. It is the *act* which counts, not the *tool*.

But in effect the objection of the Donatists to Caecilian's consecration as bishop was only a pretense. They used it although they also knew that there were a number of traditors among the bishops who had consecrated their own Maiorinus. The entire controversy was a power struggle in which the theological arguments used were, so to speak, only the stage action which would divert the audience. From the wings it looked different. Caecilian, for example, declared that he was willing to be reconsecrated by his opponents if they took offense at those who earlier had laid their hands upon him. Here was the golden opportunity for his opponents to assert and establish their theological principles, but they were not really concerned about this. Their concern was to win control of the African church. Therefore they rejected the offer of Caecilian with mocking laughter and went about organizing their own party until finally the church in Africa was divided. On the one side were Caecilian and his supporting bishops; on the other side were the Donatists and the bishops who supported them. Maiorinus had died and was succeeded by Donatus, the real spiritual head of the movement which is named after him.

All this took place before the persecution ended and in such a manner that the churches outside of Africa were unaware of the struggle. As far as non-African churches were concerned, Caecilian was the legitimate successor of Mensurius and the leader of the African church, and they maintained official relationships only with him. For this reason Constantine and his governor dealt with Caecilian until they realized from the stormy demands of the Donatists that the African church was by no means the close-knit unit which it appeared to be on the surface.

What was to be done? Synods were convened at Rome in 313 and at Arles in 314. These synods, however, accomplished little. Those who are striving for might rather than right always have their ways of evading defeat. The Donatists were condemned both at Rome and at Arles. The testimony of witnesses clearly showed that Caecilian was the rightful bishop of Africa and that the Donatist assertion that there were traditors among the bishops who had consecrated him was false. But then the Donatists simply appealed to the imperial court, and when their claims were rejected here also, they just pretended that nothing had happened. They felt strong enough to resist the state. And in fact, when Constantine attempted to support Caecilian, whose claims he considered to be legitimate, he failed because of the fanatical resistance he encountered there. He was wise enough to let the Donatists go their way, but not so his sons and their successors. Under them, bloody battles were fought, for the Donatists would not subject themselves to the demand of the state and return to the official church. The split had lasted so long that many people simply took it for granted. National viewpoints and probably social tensions as well played a role and added the fuel of passion to the fiery struggles. Rivers of blood flowed, but the church of the Donatists stood. In some places the Donatists obviously had the majority of the population on their side.

It was not until the time of Augustine that the power of the Donatists was successfully broken—but consider the means and the price! The Donatists were the clear majority in Augustine's territory; they controlled whole villages. In view of their great numbers Augustine first tried using all the eloquence at his disposal and worked against them in sermons and disputations. But none of this was effective; the dispute had long passed the stage where anything could be achieved through reason and theological discussion. In view of this, Augustine turned then to power politics and called on the state for assistance against the Donatists. Again there were tremendous revolts and heavy fighting. The more severely the state intervened, the more loudly Augustine applauded. *Cogite intrare,* "compel people to come in" (Luke 14:23) was Augustine's terrible watchword. Once more a religious disputation took place. In June of 411 a government-ordered public discussion of the issue was held between Augustine and the Donatist spokesman. Two hundred and eighty-six Catholic and two hundred and seventy-nine Donatist bishops participated in the forum. Note the strength of the Donatists! But what meaning could that have if the state, which had intervened against the Donatists, furnished the referee! Naturally Augustine was declared the victor by the imperial commissioner, and the Donatists were the vanquished. This decision furnished a new justification for persecution. The public laws against heretics had been used for a long time against the Donatists, which was completely unjust, for in doctrine they agreed completely with the Catholic church! Now their civil rights were taken from them and they were threatened with the death penalty for participating in Donatist meetings.

The history of Donatism adds a disquieting chapter to church history. In the first period the Donatists were completely in the wrong. Their origin was bedded in ignoble motives, and it is not edifying to follow their development. But the church did its utmost to repay injustice with injustice. Augustine's attitude in the controversies with the Donatists is unjustifiable even though theologically he was in the right. Within a short time the number of Donatists decreased sharply, and the rival church, which once had been so great, was only a remnant at the time of Augustine's death. Augustine believed that he had performed a great service for the church, but in reality he did it a disservice. In the battles against the Donatists, Christianity in Africa underwent an internal bankruptcy, and when in the seventh century Islam penetrated into Africa, Christianity was too weak to offer a serious, long-lasting resistance. African Christianity was hollow inwardly and fell apart, just as it had in Egypt where the church destroyed itself in a similar way, although in a different context.

ARIUS

The Influence of a Dead Heretic

Bloody and full of consequence as the Donatist controversy was, it pales in comparison to the Arian controversy. Donatism affected only the North African area; the Arian controversy involved the whole church, first in the East, later, especially when the Germanic tribes began to become an important factor, in the West. Whereas the Donatist controversy was primarily a power struggle, the Arian controversy went to the heart of theology and could have had a radical effect on the form of the church. Of course, human motives played a part in the Arian controversy also, especially in its later stages when church-state relationships became involved. Generally speaking, however, the Arian controversy involved two fundamentally different conceptions of Christianity.

Arius and Athanasius were the personalities who, according to the traditional view, were the central figures in this controversy. This view is only partially correct. First of all, Athanasius did not play a role at all at the outset; later on he played only a subordinate role. Even at the time of the Council of Nicaea he was only a deacon and participated in the council only as a companion of Bishop Alexander of Alexandria. The latter was at first the opponent of Arius. And Arius, the pastor at the Baucalis Church in Alexandria, was involved in the controversy not as an individual but as a representative of a theological school, that of Antioch. The reason for Arius' centrality in the controversy belongs to the complicated story of Egypt's internal controversies, something which cannot be dealt with here.

The controversy began as a dispute between Arius and his superior, Bishop Alexander. Arius was denounced to the bishop by the Melitians, who were anything but favorable to the bishop. This party took pleasure in forcing the bishop to call Arius, who once had belonged to their party but then "defected" to the bishop, to account. If Arius had not gone over to Alexander, the Melitians probably would not have taken offense at his theological views, even though they differed from their own. But now they professed profound indignity and outrage at the views of Arius, who followed in the theological tradition of Dionysius of Alexandria, who had once sharply stressed the difference between God the Father and the Son. The Melitians' beliefs were more akin to those of the people who at one time had accused Dionysius in Rome. Alexander himself stood in the tradition of Origen, and even though his tradition was different from that of Arius, he was really closer to Arius than to the Melitians. Although Alexander had little love for the Melitians, after the denunciation he had no other choice but to take action against Arius. He probably would much rather have left Arius alone. Besides, he did not take the heresy of Arius as seriously as did the Melitians.

It soon became apparent that Alexander would have been wiser to leave Arius undisturbed. But by this time, the bishop was no longer able to turn back. Indeed, the synods he convened solemnly condemned Arius, but Arius' congregation did not even think of expelling its pastor, who had been deposed. And those who shared Arius' theological point of view were vigorous in supporting him. These sympathizers were not satisfied with sending protests to Alexander; they convened synods on their own initiative, and these synods approved the theological views of Arius. Even worse for Alexander was the fact that these synods revoked the deposition of Arius. With such support coming from outside quarters, the party of Arius in Alexandria became more and more active, finally provoking unrest in the city and the election of a counter-bishop in opposition to Alexander. The incumbent bishop defended himself as best he could; but he could not outmaneuver his opponents, either in the field of theology or in church politics.

Bishop Alexander did not live to see the end of the controversy which was now spreading beyond his diocese. It was his successor Athanasius who continued the struggle against Arius. Although the friends of Arius were powerful, and although even the emperor lent him support, he did not have the satisfaction of seeing his cause victorious. Instead the Council of Nicaea expelled him from Alexandria, and he spent the rest of his life in exile (the sources are not completely clear about this). Shortly before he was to be solemnly reinstated, he died suddenly on a street in Constantinople in the year 336. Several times he had been assured that he would be reinstated, but it never happened.

Very little can be said about the personality of Arius because his opponents' hostility not only caused the destruction of his works but also made it impossible to arrive at a true picture of his life and work. So far as posterity is concerned, Arius was an arch-heretic. A tragic combination of unhappy coincidences has made him such. Arius was neither the founder nor the spiritual leader of the theological school which was attacked in his person. No doubt the controversy named after him would have taken place without him; the issue was unavoidable. Had the Melitians not denounced him, Arius perhaps would have stood completely on the periphery of church history.

The doctrine which he advocated was rightly rejected, but for a long time it continued to play a significant role in the church. Only twenty years after Arius' death his views practically determined the imperial policy toward the church even though his name was not mentioned and he was still regarded as an excommunicated heretic. The court bishops used formulae which, despite their avoidance of Arius' expressions, still favored his intentions. And yet another twenty years later, in the last years of Emperor Valens, the influence of Arius' views was still determinative for imperial policy. But the tide was beginning to turn, as became apparent somewhat later under Emperor Theodosius I. The anti-Arian forces faced much opposition; but in Constantinople, for instance, Gregory of Nazianzus could be appointed bishop of the city only in face of bitter resistance by the enraged crowds. By the end of the fourth century Arianism was almost dead in the Roman Empire, but the Germans were hammering at the gates of Rome. Emperor Theodosius was still able to contain the Germanic Goths, but his successor was not. They flooded over the empire, and with them Arianism staged a comeback. The Gothic apostle Ulfilas (died A.D. 383) had been consecrated bishop by an Arian. After the Goths, one Germanic tribe after the other accepted Christianity in its Arian form.

Thus for more than a hundred years Arian churches existed on Roman soil. And these Germanic national churches gave the Catholic church great anxiety, until finally, in the sixth century, their strength abated and Catholicism again predominated in the Roman Empire and was able to extend its missions far beyond Italy into German territory.

ATHANASIUS

Christ — Creature or Eternal Son?

For a number of years the Arian controversy disturbed not only the Egyptian church, but almost the whole Eastern church. Thus, when the Eastern Empire came under the rule of Constantine in 324, he was confronted by a situation similar to the one he had encountered in Africa, where the Donatist controversy had taken place: the Christian church was split and disunited. Here, too, the emperor sought to intervene as a peacemaker between the opposing parties. Imperial diplomacy and local synods, however, had only a limited success. Then Constantine took a great risk. He convened a synod of the empire, an ecumenical council. Only few bishops came from the West, not because of the geographical distance alone, but because the Western church was not really concerned with the questions that were to be debated.

In the summer of the year 325, bishops began to arrive in Nicaea from all the areas of the East. They traveled by imperial coach and were accorded every courtesy. What a change had come about in the way Christians were treated! The council met in the imperial palace, housed and fed at public expense. Constantine himself participated in its deliberations. After considerable discussion the council agreed on a formula which was to be signed by all participants as a statement of what they held in common on the relationship of the Father to the Son. Arius and two of his sympathizers were excommunicated, and the matter appeared to be settled.

But this was not the case. It became clear that Nicaea had only covered up, not settled, the questions at stake. Earlier there had been three views on the relationship of the Father and the Son. No one any longer advocated the old Monarchianism (at least not with the formulas and reasons used earlier), but the matter as such still remained to be dealt with. Christ was spoken of as the incarnate Logos of the Father, but that, too, was just a formula which might be used as a cover for old ideas. We therefore see a theological right wing which considered Christ as practically identical with the Father, just as before. It was recognized that a distinction had to be made between the two, but this remained mere theory. In practice Christ was identical with God. For how could man be saved except by being drawn into the Godhead through fellowship with Christ? The more Christ was distinguished from the Father, it was asserted, the more his divinity was lessened and man's salvation endangered.

The old Monarchians, popular piety, and Athanasius were united in the struggle against any such subordinating view. To the extent that the West gave any thought to the matter, this is where the Western church also stood.

Opposite this right wing there was a left wing which, just as Dionysius of Alexandria had done somewhat earlier, distinguished the Son so strongly from the Father that he practically became a being subordinate to the Father. If God is the origin of all things, then there must have been a time when he was alone, a time when he did not have the Son at his side. And then there must have been a time when the Son was created by the Father. According to this, Father and Son were both God, but not in the same way. In the fullest sense of the word the Father alone is God, the Son is subordinate to him, a creature of the Father like all others, although basically distinguished from them. This is what Arius taught and it is substantially the view held by his friends and the Arians of the later period. They rightfully claimed Origen as the source of their views.

A third group, which we would like to call the central party, also proceeded from Origen and drew on him for support when it distinguished the Son from the Father. This party, however, played down the differences between Father and Son in such a way that the difference between them is only a theoretical one. There was always the Trinity, indivisible, unchangeable, and immutable, according to Gregory Thaumatourgos, one of the spokesmen of this central party, which, building on Origen, moved in the direction of the right wing.

The emperor's attempt to work out a solution at Nicaea which would bring all three groups to a common position was destined to failure because Constantine used insufficient means. He attempted to override instead of to convince, and he exerted his personal authority in questions which demanded theological solutions. Thus we see that after 325 things were more confused than before. Left and right wing persistently maintained their original convictions. The center group changed its position somewhat, for it drew support from those who originally had supported Arius; thus this party became stronger. Now this party began to pull together those who had taken positions both to the left and right of Origen; it combined them on a middle course and actually advanced the theological attempt to grasp the nature of the deity in a way that would not sacrifice theological integrity to practical or pietistic demands. Every Eastern theologian of any standing belonged to this party which moved energetically away from the agreement of Nicaea. For all practical purposes Constantine favored this party, for almost all his ecclesiastical advisors belonged to it. If the theology of this party, at least at first, did not meet with complete acceptance, it was due to Athanasius, against whom the struggle of the Anti-Nicaeans was mostly directed.

Following the death of Alexander, Athanasius was consecrated bishop of Alexandria on June 8, 328. But his elevation to the episcopate was attended by difficulty, for in addition to the Arian controversy, the church in Egypt was still torn by the ecclesio-political conflict between the Melitians and the official church, which up to this time had been led by Alexander. Both Arians and Melitians readily attacked Athanasius. But Athanasius was not to be outdone by his opponents in anything—neither in craftiness, in violence nor in eloquence. Athanasius was not made of the stuff of which saints are made. Today he is wrongly portrayed as the ideal fighter against the tutelage of the church by the state. Nevertheless it is impressive to see how he stood up to all difficulties.

At the beginning of the year 332 Athanasius was ordered for the first time to appear before the emperor for questioning, but he acquitted himself masterfully. Shortly afterward, Constantine commanded him to receive Arius into the fellowship of the Egyptian church (which shows how successfully the battle against the decision of Nicaea had progressed), but Athanasius flatly refused. In 333 a new investigation against Athanasius was undertaken, but due to the bishop's skill the investigation got nowhere. In the following year a synod met to take action against him, but Athanasius refused to appear before this body. In 335 another synod convened, before which he had to appear. But when the deliberations ran unfavorably for him, he secretly left the convention and sought out the emperor. While his power and eloquence were succeeding in winning over the emperor, who was at first unfavorably disposed, his opponents were unleashing their strongest weapon and accusing Athanasius of political troublemaking. With that weapon they succeeded in having Athanasius banished to Treves, on the border of the empire.

When Constantine died in 337, Athanasius was permitted to return to Alexandria. But his stay there was not long. Constantine's sons divided the empire into three parts. After the third son of the great Constantine, Constantine II, died in battle against his brother Constans, the latter ruled the West alone, so that then there were only two parts. Constantius, who ruled the Eastern Empire, was won over to the side of Athanasius' opponents. In 339 Athanasius had to flee from Alexandria where, after bloody tumults, a counter-bishop was enthroned. He found refuge in the West. Here the Roman pope, Julius, not only made the cause of Athanasius his own, but the ruler of the West, Constans, also interceded for him. Thus Athanasius was able to return again to Alexandria after seven long years of exile. Constantius considered it more prudent not to resist this turn of events.

But even now Athanasius' stay was not permanent. Constans, who was not popular with the people, was deposed by a rebellion in the year 350 and finally murdered. With that Constantius became the sole ruler. As soon as he had subjected the rebels and held the West solidly in his hand, Constantius, who had been forced to occasional compromise out of regard for Constans, reverted to his former policy toward the church and went even further. Previously the emperor had followed the line of the central party; now he followed the advice of those who persuaded him toward the line of Arius' thinking. Naturally they did not do this explicitly, but the formulations they used led to a position close to that of original Arianism. One of their first aims was to deal energetically with Athanasius. Constantius used the means at his disposal to put the Western church under pressure, until, with only few exceptions, the bishops consented to Athanasius' condemnation. Those few who opposed this action were forced into exile. In the whole empire only one man still resisted successfully —Athanasius! An imperial officer sent out against him had to withdraw from Alexandria without success. A police action was thwarted because of the resistance of the congregation. Only when the military was dispatched against him and marched into Alexandria in 356, did Athanasius give in. He fled, as previously in the year 339, this time into a hiding place in Egypt, since even the Western part of the empire no longer offered him refuge.

The common people continued to resist for more than three months, until the churches were finally vacated by force and turned over to the opponents of Athanasius. With blatant force his adherents were persecuted. The outraged population arose in rebellion and took the life of the counter-bishop, but this did not change the situation. The actions of the emperor became sharper and more energetic. Until now the Roman pope, Liberius, had resisted joining in the condemnation of Athanasius which was demanded of him and was himself banished for his refusal, but now he vacillated also. He condemned Athanasius and bowed to the will of Constantius just as did the synod of Rimini, where over four hundred bishops of the West were gathered, at first all solidly determined to resist the emperor's will to renew, although indirectly, the heresy of Arius. But the bishops were not permitted to return to their homes until, one after the other, they capitulated and declared that the opinion held by the theologians of the East and the emperor was theirs also.

In fact, the theologians of the East were not as Arian-minded as was asserted. Many of them held an opinion quite different from that of the emperor and his court bishops, and they stressed the equality in the nature of God the Father and the Son as well as the difference between them. But they were unable to defend and assert themselves until Constantius died in 361 on an expedition against Julian, who had risen in rebellion. Now the entire picture was changed.

Julian was anything but a friend of the Christians, but despite this—or perhaps just because of it—his initial policy toward the church was friendly. His policy was equal rights for all ecclesiastical movements and tolerance for all opinions. All who had been banished, whether Athanasians or Arians, were permitted to return, were reinstated in their offices, and told to live peacefully with their opponents. This often led to remarkable situations. For instance, in Alexandria we see an Arian bishop executing his office beside Athanasius, who had returned in triumph in 362. However, this situation was short-lived, for after a few months Athanasius had to leave the city again, not because Julian favored the Arians, but because the bishop became too troublesome for the emperor.

This banishment was short, for Julian's reign, which had turned a hostile face toward Christianity, passed quickly. Therefore, in February of 364 Athanasius returned to Alexandria. Nor was this latest banishment the last one. Under Julian's successors Athanasius was once again exiled from the city for a few months. But after that he spent his remaining years in peace. The ecclesiastical horizon was still overcast (the new emperors continued to pursue a policy favorable to Arianism) but Athanasius had peace until his death on May 3, 373. Even in his last years he followed ecclesiastical events attentively and participated actively in them. Frequently he was asked for advice since he was the patriarch who had stood almost for fifty years in the fore of the battles for the divinity of Jesus Christ. However, it was not granted to Athanasius to find the salutary words which would have ended the struggle. But the position he fought for was sound, for the theology of Arius would have led to consequences which might have destroyed the Christian's certainty of salvation.

According to Arianism, Christ was still only a creature; the Trinity was lowered to the temporal realm; and Jesus was not the Savior but the teacher who brought the knowledge that would lead men to God. It was against this that Athanasius had defended the divinity of Jesus Christ for the sake of the salvation of mankind. This concern, which was also the concern of the Christian congregations, should have been formulated in such a way that it fitted into the theological picture as a whole and made possible a vivid picture of the unity of the divine Trinity of Father, Son, and Holy Spirit without saying too much or too little about any one of the three Persons.

Athanasius, even in his advanced years, was incapable of formulating that, even though he had the rare ability to understand not only his own concerns, but those of his opponents as well. Athanasius was a stalwart fighter, but he was not a theologian in the true sense. He was nearly helpless in the face of the new developments that sprang up in the last decades of his life and was unable, for instance, to give a helping hand to Basil of Caesarea, who held out the solution which made it possible to end the Arian controversy, at least so far as it can be said that such a controversy has ever ended.

EUSEBIUS OF CAESAREA

Father of Church History

The name of Eusebius of Caesarea has been mentioned quite frequently in these pages. It is simply impossible to write any kind of account of the history of the church during the first three centuries without resorting again and again to the works of Eusebius. His *Church History* gives us access to a host of sources and traditions otherwise long since lost. Eusebius had the treasures of the past at his disposal in unique measure, and he knew how to make use of them. Origen had already laid the foundation for the library at Caesarea when he was forced to leave Alexandria and take up residence in Palestine. Pamphilus, an enthusiastic adherent of Origen, had added to the library and continued the teaching ministry of Origen. Eusebius, the pupil, co-worker, and friend of Pamphilus, became his successor when Pamphilus died as a martyr in the Diocletian persecution. He knew how to make use of his inheritance and justly deserved his reputation for scholarship, which his hostile contemporaries and the polemicism of later generations minimized for a time, but could never seriously impair.

As a follower of Origen, Eusebius naturally took the side of the opponents of the Nicene Council and of Athanasius in the Arian controversy, and often intervened on behalf of Arius. For this he was condemned by the synod of Antioch in 324. The Council of Nicaea, however, reversed this sentence, for by this time Eusebius had achieved an extremely influential position. Not only had he become bishop of Caesarea, but soon after the cessation of the Diocletian persecution, he was also held in high regard by Emperor Constantine. At about the time he assumed the office of bishop, Eusebius published a series of writings, among them his chronicle of the world and, most important, his account of the church's history from the days of the apostles to the end of the Diocletian persecution. Later he continued the account in several editions. "I am not aware that any Christian writer has until now paid attention to this type of writing," Eusebius correctly wrote in his introduction, for this was something completely new, and Constantine, no doubt, recognized immediately the significance such a man would have. He selected Eusebius as his scholarly mentor. Eusebius showed his appreciation for this appointment by praising the emperor in both speeches and writings. These writings are among our most important sources of knowledge about Constantine and his age.

These laudatory works of Eusebius brought him little gratitude from posterity. In reference to them, Jacob Burckhardt called Eusebius the "most disgusting of all flatterers" and "the first completely insincere historian of antiquity." These harsh words have been in circulation for a hundred years and have found an echo. Are they valid? Definitely not! Burckhardt's evaluation of Eusebius is obviously anything but impartial. His conception of Constantine and the Constantinian era is quite the opposite of that of Eusebius. That is completely understandable, considering their totally different presuppositions. But even if Burckhardt's views were correct, which is not at all the case, it is contrary to historical thinking to expect Eusebius, at the beginning of the fourth century, to have the viewpoint of the nineteenth century.

Burckhardt accuses Eusebius of trying to make Constantine "at any price an ideal of humanity in his sense, especially an ideal of future princes." In so doing, Burckhardt says, Eusebius distorted the image of Constantine. But even this is by no means correct. If one reads Eusebius with an open mind, one cannot fail to realize that he is not at all blind to the darker side of Constantine's life and character. That is why Eusebius foregoes treating the political and military deeds of Constantine and restricts himself to examples of the emperor's "pious life," something which he can praise with a good conscience. Everything else Eusebius passes over with an eloquent silence. It would be unreasonable to expect ruthless criticism of the emperor by Eusebius. Certainly nineteenth-century historians, under circumstances similar to those that existed for Constantine and Eusebius, were no harsher in their criticisms of their rulers.

It is probably inaccurate to assume that Eusebius was silent about untoward aspects of Constantine's life out of fear, although in view of the totalitarian and bloody regime of the emperor's sons, great caution was very appropriate. Gratitude and respect restrained Eusebius from speaking. Constantine was the man who brought about the great turning point of the world and who gave freedom to the Christian church. That was what stuck in the minds of Christians in that age. And that is what stuck in the mind of Eusebius and governed his portrayal of the life of Constantine. It was not until after the death of the emperor that Eusebius took pen in hand; he did not write as did the flatterers of his time in order to acquire the gratitude of a living monarch! Nor did he write to ingratiate himself with Constantine's sons. As a matter of fact, he wrote the book in advanced age, and died a short time later.

His work was an expression of the gratitude felt by all Christians of the fourth century to Constantine for what he had done. No doubt he exaggerated somewhat, but we have no reason to condemn him for that as Burckhardt and others have done. Indeed, Burckhardt and his followers had no appreciation of the historical value of the documents which Eusebius so generously wove into his biography. With the passing of time, Burckhardt's widely circulated argument against Eusebius has proved untenable. We have every reason to be grateful to Eusebius for his work, even though we have some reservation about some of his judgments.

Eusebius was the most important historian of Christian antiquity. The writing of church history as such begins with him, and none of the historical writers in the following generation can be compared with him. Neither Gelasius nor Rufinus, nor Socrates, Sozomen, Theodoret or whatever their names, can compare with him. Yet his activity as a historian was only a small part of his theological and literary work. Eusebius defended Christianity by writing apologetical treatises against pagans and Jews. In scholarly commentaries he interpreted many passages of the Old Testament. He acquired renown in regard to the text of the Bible. Much more could be mentioned—his letters and sermons, his dogmatic writings (Eusebius was one of the foremost theological thinkers of his time), his investigation of the differences between the Gospels, his list of biblical place names, and more.

But all this must remain out of consideration for the present. We just want to add a word about his writing in connection with the martyrs in Palestine. In eleven chapters Eusebius gives a comprehensive picture of the sufferings endured by Christians during the years of the Diocletian persecution in his own home province of Palestine. The eighth book of his *Church History* contains supplements to this description. In reading this attentively, the attitude of fourth-century Christians toward Constantine can be better understood. It is easy to criticize the Constantinian era and perhaps to pass judgment on the bishops who gave in to the wishes of the emperor at the council of Nicaea and afterward. But anyone who has studied in depth the conditions which existed before Constantine's accession and who has a clear picture of the years of gruesome terror which the Christians had to undergo will not judge these men too quickly.

A new epoch began with the sons of Constantine, and here other judgments must apply. If the memory of the time of persecution was still uppermost in the minds of the bishops and of the church as a whole and influenced their attitude toward Constantine to such an extent that they yielded to the emperor as the tool obviously given by God, then these are motives for which only those people who think unhistorically or who are inclined to make pharisaic judgments will have no understanding. On the other hand, the attitude of many Christians during the age of Constantine's sons, the age when the imperial church was in the process of formation, was determined by real weakness and fear of men. One cannot make excuses for their behavior, and judgment upon them must be rendered with severity.

ANTHONY

Hermit of the Desert

It was Jesus' words to the rich young man (Matt. 19:21) that
directed Anthony on his way to monasticism. He, too, was a
young man, perhaps not rich, but still, he could live without
worry on what his father had left him. But unlike the young man
in the Gospel, Anthony decided to separate himself from the
world and he wasted no time in doing so. He turned his land-
holdings over to the farmers of his Egyptian home village, sold all
his movable goods, and gave the proceeds to the poor. He lodged
his sister in a house of Christian maidens. Freed of family re-
sponsibilities which had tied him to the past and to the bourgeois
life, he now dedicated himself fully to the matter of the salvation
of his soul.

The decision was not difficult for him to reach. There were
many examples of such renunciation for Anthony to follow. In
the Egypt of the waning third century (if the tradition is reliable,
these things took place around 275) in the environs of not a few
villages men could be found who isolated themselves from society
in order to live without disturbance for the salvation of their souls.
Anthony sought them out to learn from them. He took for himself something from each and combined it into a system of rigorous
severity. He passed many sleepless nights, and when he did sleep,
he did so only on bare ground, and in the most extreme case,

on a bed of rushes. He waited until evening before he took his one meal of the day, which consisted of bread and salt. But often he did not eat anything for two, three, even four days in a row. Far away from his native village and from people, he settled among the graves. Very infrequently one of his acquaintances would come and provide him with bread.

One morning an acquaintance found Anthony lying on the ground, apparently dead. He picked him up and carried him into the village church, where friends and relatives came to mourn his death. But around midnight Anthony revived and had himself secretly taken back to his place of contemplation. The demons had been able to inflict bodily injury on him, but his inner strength was unbroken. Now the devil with all his legions attacked him again. The tomb in which Anthony lived shook from their noise. They appeared to him as lions, bears, wild steers, and wolves, and threatened to tear him to pieces. But Anthony remained fearless. Then a light shone, and in the splendor of this light the demons became invisible and the pain in the tortured body ceased. The voice of the Lord called to Anthony: "Anthony, I was here, but I was waiting to see you struggle. Since you endured the struggle without succumbing, I will always help you and I will make you famous in all places."

At this time Anthony was about thirty-five years of age. The appearance of the light awakened new powers in him. He went into the desert to serve God and there to fight against the demons. He settled in a deserted citadel and hoped to be able to remain there completely alone. But soon people found their way to him. Just as he once had gone to other hermits to learn from them, now disciples gathered around him to imitate his example. At the time he went into the desert there was yet no organized settlement of hermits, for they were accustomed to live more or less close to inhabited areas. Even Anthony's teacher had refused to go with him. Now the desert was populated with men who, like Anthony, had cut completely the ties between themselves and society, and Anthony was their example and teacher.

In time even the company of these hermits became a burden for him. When the needs of his body forced him to eat, he was ashamed of his dependence on bodily things and went far away so that no one would see him take food. He was especially disturbed by the curious, who made pilgrimages to him either to admire him or to seek a cure for their sicknesses of body and soul at his hand. These people distracted him from the struggle of cleansing his own soul of everything earthly.

After living for twenty years in the company of hermits he finally escaped into the remotest desert where he even made himself independent of support by others. Until now bread had been brought to him, even if at long intervals. In his new environment, a mountain removed by three days travel from the former place of activity, he sowed grain and became free of any human support. In ceaseless prayer he served God and fought against the demons, who were forced to yield to him despite all their efforts to overcome him. The saint who brought God such extraordinary sacrifices was rewarded by him with miraculous gifts.

When Anthony had moved into the deserted citadel twenty years before, all the vermin left. Now just a word of exhortation to the beasts of the desert who damaged his grain crop was sufficient to keep them away for ever. His prayers made water flow from the dry ground. He could perceive what took place far away. Invalids who did not shy away from the rigor of a journey to him were healed. But his miraculous power was effective even at great distances.

Yet Anthony was a model of orthodoxy. He was subject to the bishops and free of pride and arrogance toward the clergy of the church. He despised all worldly education and stated: "He whose mind is sound does not need scholarship." He effortlessly won debates with philosophers and doubters who sought him out to test their wisdom on him.

Thus decade after decade passed until he was 105 years old; then he prepared to take leave of the world. Two sheepskins and one cloak were his only earthly possessions. He left them to the bishops

Athanasius and Sarapion. His last concern before death was that his body be buried in an unmarked and secret grave. Then he closed his eyes.

What we have presented here is based on Athanasius' report of the life of Anthony, the founder of hermit life in Egypt. A short time after Anthony's death in the year 356, Athanasius wrote this biography or legend of a saint as a guide and exhortation for the monks of Egypt, who in the meantime had become quite numerous. It had the intended influence then, but still more important was the effect it had on later centuries. Augustine, Francis of Assisi, and numerous others were led on the way paved by Anthony to a conscious and sacrificial Christian life.

PACHOMIUS

Founder of Monasticism

Who was the first Christian monk? According to Athanasius of Alexandria it was Anthony the hermit. According to Jerome, in one of his biographies of the monks, it was Paul of Thebes. One may debate to what extent fiction and fact vie with each other in the biography of Anthony by Athanasius, but there is general agreement that Jerome's report is a product of pure literary fantasy. The biography of Anthony became famous instantaneously; as soon as it became known it was read avidly. Jerome begrudged both Anthony and Athanasius this fame, hence his competitive writing.

No doubt there were hermits in Egypt before Anthony. This is clear from the report of Anthanasius about him. But Anthony gave hermit life its characteristic form. The description of his life by Athanasius played just as large a role as the efforts of Anthony himself in the development of the hermit or monastic life. The colonies of hermits which sprang up in the first half of the fourth century in various places in Egypt can be traced to a large extent directly or indirectly back to his example. Each monk lived alone in his own cell. The cells were so far apart that one monk was unable to hear or see his neighbor. The monks came together only for religious services. They earned their livelihood by braiding mats, a purely mechanical activity which was chosen deliberately because in this way the monk was not distracted by his work from prayer and contemplation.

The monk had only one concern, the salvation of his soul. Here we are confronted with a most impressive striving for holiness, the reasons for which are not very difficult to find. Once Christianity came to power, it was in danger of becoming increasingly secularized. Emperor Constantine had begun to favor the church with very substantial gifts and endowments, and each succeeding generation added new wealth to the church's coffers. The bishops had become influential lords whose word carried weight even in the highest political circles. It was advisable to be a Christian if one wanted to get ahead in his profession. And the church found all this good! It had become a part of this world, completely in opposition to its real destiny.

It was then that the pious fled from the world and even from the church into solitude. They thought that only in isolation could they be safe from the temptation which lay in ambush all around them. The hermit chastised himself; he made fewer and fewer concessions to the demands of his body; he believed these things would bring him closer to God. Every contact with men was regarded by him as an obstacle in his search for detachment from the world. Anthony went deeper and deeper into the desert because he objected to every disturbance of his solitude, even though such disturbance came from disciples or those seeking help of some kind. This was an obstacle to his own salvation, for—and that is the limit of this asceticism—the hermit is concerned only with himself. At work here is a holy egotism which concentrates all of the individual's powers in an astonishing measure, but only for his own salvation. Despite the magnificence of this tremendous effort, it loses sight of the true goal of Christianity. A Christian who thinks only of his own salvation and is not concerned about the salvation of his neighbor has forgotten the central motive of Christianity. Thus even the greatest effort of these holy men— which they were without doubt—must seem in vain to us.

In the following period the degree of Anthony's asceticism was surpassed. There were monks who restricted themselves voluntarily to a certain place. They went only from their cell to the church nearby or they had themselves walled in. Others took up their abode on mountaintops and renounced even shelter over their heads. The so-called pillar saints pushed asceticism to its ulti- mate extreme. One of them, whose life is fully described to us, had himself buried for two years. He then climbed to a mountain- top where he lived inside a narrow wall, anchored by an iron chain, under the open sky. He spent the next five years on a rock about four feet high. He had more and more rocks placed on top of each other until finally the construction of a pillar was necessary. This also grew higher and higher until, for the final thirty years, he lived on a pillar about seventy feet in height, exposed to all the inclemencies of weather and immersed in constant prayer. He is not unique; there were a number of these "pillar saints" during the fourth and fifth centuries.

From Egypt this hermit life rapidly spread in its various forms into all the Christian churches of the East. But not only this form of asceticism, which can be admired even though it horrifies us, but also the system of monasteries as we know it came from Egypt. Pachomius was the founder of the latter.

Born of pagan parents, he came into contact with Christians for the first time during his period as a military recruit. Pressed into the military service by force and, according to the custom of the time, treated inhumanely as a recruit, he himself experienced the active Christian love of neighbor. This event obviously caused him to become a Christian. For, as he tells us in his autobiography, he rejoined these Christians as soon as he was released from military service. He received their instruction with zeal. In a dream on the night after his baptism he had a vision which promised him the special grace of Christ. Thus Pachomius became a monk, for to be a Christian in the true sense meant in those days to become a monk.

Like Anthony, Pachomius also went into apprenticeship to one of the hermits of the area. But his path took a different turn from Anthony's. According to a contemporary tradition, he received a direct command from God. This divine command ordered him to found a monastery and gave him detailed regulations for it. In the biography of Pachomius, as in that of Anthony, we find many later pious additions, and no doubt this story about a divine command is one of them. Obviously there were monasteries before Pachomius' time, organized similarly to those founded by him, but they were only a small beginning. Pachomius is the real founder of the cloistered life. Very soon numerous monasteries were organized along the lines of his original monastery. And from Egypt the form originated by him spread into other lands.

A monastery of Pachomius looked quite similar to its modern counterpart: a wall closed the monastery building off from the outside world. Each monk was assigned to a certain building in which he had his individual cell containing his few possessions. All monks were to have an occupation. Either they engaged in a trade or else they cultivated the land on which the monastery was located. In addition, service was rendered to the community. In the morning and evening the house fellowships met for communal worship. The hours between were filled with work which was done for the good of the monastery fellowship; the products of the house fellowships were sold for the benefit of the monastery. Asceticism was valued highly, but wise moderation kept it within appropriate limits. The whole fellowship was characterized by the principle of voluntarism, and everyone was examined carefully before he was admitted.

This form of monasticism is more familiar to us. But even here its limits are clearly visible. The Bible played an important role; it was learned by heart, and the more Scripture a monk could recite from memory, the more respected he was. But the role of the Bible stopped at this external memorization. It was the same with prayer. The more prayers a monk knew and the more often he prayed, the more saintly he was considered. But this praying was a mechanical recital. The sacrament was valued highly, and a service without Holy Communion was unthinkable. But this had no true significance for the monks' striving after salvation. The monks were very careful to stay within the designated form of church doctrine. But this also was no more than an external agreement. The most prized element in monasticism was the achievement of the will, the exertion of the moral strength of the monk. Through it the monk expected to achieve salvation. And it is true of the monasticism of Pachomius that man, the neighbor in the world, was completely outside of the view of the monks. The monk was concerned only for his own soul's salvation, not that of his neighbor. And even the thought that one could also serve God in the world was completely alien to him.

From the fourth century on we find monasticism throughout the Christian church of the East. Monastery fellowship and the hermit's cell are found side by side yet without any contact. On the other hand, in the West monasticism spread slowly and with great resistance. Everywhere there could be found groups of pious people who devoted themselves quietly to the practice of asceticism. Jerome and Rufinus, Ambrose and Augustine set the example for this. But people looked with distrust on these things, and again and again the more secular spirit of the West rebelled against it. Only Martin of Tours in Gaul and the disciples of Augustine in Africa helped monasticism take root in the West. It was Benedict of Nursia who led Western monasticism to its first true blossoming.

JULIAN THE APOSTATE

Lapsed Christian—Last Pagan

It was Emperor Constantine who put an end to the persecution of the Christian church and gave Christianity equal rights with the other religions of the Roman Empire. As we stated in our earlier treatment of Constantine, there can be no doubt that he was a Christian by faith and inner conviction. Nonetheless, he felt forced to follow a cautious policy toward paganism, for the majority of his subjects, especially the nobility and the upper classes, still worshiped the old gods. Of course, many of them were only externally loyal to the old gods, but they were still far removed from a conversion to Christianity.

From the moment Constantine's sons, Constantius, Constans, and Constantine II came to power, the religious policy of the state changed. If the population could still be in doubt about Constantine's personal Christianity, there could be no doubt about that of his sons. Christianity now became the imperial church, and paganism, once so overpowering, was pushed more and more back on the defensive. In the year 341, four years after the death of Constantine, pagan sacrifices were prohibited. In the year 354 the closing of all pagan temples was ordered, and finally, in 356, not only service and sacrifice but also any veneration of the idols were made subject to stringent penalties. Even though the execution of these anti-pagan edicts was less severe than the decrees themselves, the policy which the state and its rulers followed was unambiguously clear.

The rule of the gods seemed to be at an end. But the triumph of the Christians lasted only a short time. By the year 361 pagan temples were opened again everywhere, pagan festivals were solemnly celebrated, sacrifices were offered to the gods, the priests were reinstated in their positions of honor, and confiscated temple properties were restored. On the other hand, churches were closed and the pagan population which had previously been relegated to the background and occasionally mistreated by the Christians took their revenge, going as far as to murder some bishops, as was the case in Alexandria. The reign of Emperor Julian had begun.

"Julian the Apostate" he has been called since that time, and succeeding centuries have never tired of heaping abuse upon him. He had defected from Christianity, in which he grew up, and returned to paganism. At one time he had read the Gospel as a lector (a member of the lower clergy) in the services, but now he was not satisfied with just participating in pagan sacrifice. He even performed the sacrifice himself and honored those who, despite the unfavorable condition of the preceding times, had stood fast in paganism or had, like himself, defected from Christianity to paganism.

How could this be possible? We have to go back into the childhood of Julian to find the reasons. Even his father's boyhood had been marked by threatening pressure. His father was a brother of Emperor Constantine and therefore forced to extreme self-control lest he awaken the distrust of Constantine the Great, who, when angered, did not spare even his own family. Constantine had had his son Crispus and his wife Fausta murdered—probably in a moment of jealousy. Toward the end of his life Constantine was more mildly inclined toward his brothers, but hardly had he closed his eyes when his three sons had all the remaining male members of the family killed. Julian and his brother Gallus were the only ones who escaped this bloodbath—Gallus because he was sick at the time, and Julian because he was just six years old and also because, as a presumably trustworthy report has it, Christian clergymen took care of him and spirited him out of the palace into the protection of a church.

Julian, then, grew up without parents, for his mother had died shortly after his birth. He lived in hiding, completely occupied with his studies. Nevertheless, his father's fate repeated itself in Julian. Constantius, who at first had taken over the rule in the East but then brought the whole empire under his sway, followed his steps with suspicious distrust. Nowhere was Julian free; nowhere could he completely be himself. As pious as Constantius pretended to be his life was not that of a Christian emperor. The mixture of Christian words and unchristian deeds, the mendacity at court, the corruption among the servants—all this made it impossible for Julian to see his cousin Constantius as much of an example. No extenuating circumstances could shake Julian's conviction that it was the Christian Emperor Constantius who had had his father murdered. And the murder of his father and of all his relatives was followed by the murder of his brother Gallus. The empire was split; the Christian church was torn asunder by theological controversies. One bishop condemned the other. Each one had arguments to defend his position, but where was the truth?

In his studies Julian found the clarity he was seeking. Customarily education took place by exposing the youth to the writings of the Greek poets and philosophers. Most young men of that time went through this education without damage. They remained untouched by the contents of the literature that was held before them as an example, and they learned only from its form. But with Julian it was different. He was completely taken with Greek philosophy. He became more and more at home in Greek life until finally, initiated into the secrets of the Greek mystery cults, he was a Christian only outwardly. In reality he was just waiting for the opportunity to get rid of the burdensome fetters of Christianity.

The opportunity soon presented itself. The empire, at one time held together by the firm hand of Constantine, had in the meantime fallen into serious difficulties under Constantius. The Persians threatened in the East, the Germans in the West. Constantius himself wanted to lead the fight against the Persians, but he needed a member of his own family to act as his representative in the West, since in faraway Gaul disturbances and rebellions had broken out too often. Julian was the only one who was available, and despite his distrust of him, Constantius sent Julian to the German border. He thought he would be able to guide the inexperienced young man by means of advisers (actually, supervisors) whom he would appoint. At the age of twenty-four Julian was solemnly elevated as Caesar (that is, a kind of crown prince), and sent to Gaul, a province which was threatened by repeated German invasions and which was internally weakened by the mismanagement of the emperor and his officials. It is astonishing how quickly and thoroughly Julian mastered his new tasks. In the briefest time he became a commander in chief who was able to restore the old awe of Roman power in the border province. Step by step the Germans were pushed back and the old fortresses restored. The completely corrupt administration was newly organized, the almost unbearable tax burden of the people was made lighter until finally all of Gaul had been reconquered externally and internally.

Constantius viewed the successes of Julian with concern, and very quickly a conflict developed between them. When the Persian danger reached a new zenith, Constantius demanded reinforcements from Gaul. He wanted Julian's best troops for himself. But the regiments mutinied; they did not want to go to the far East, nor did they want to be separated from Julian. They proclaimed Julian emperor, and civil war seemed imminent. But before an armed conflict developed between the two cousins, Constantius died.

The empire was in the hands of Julian. And now, he believed, was the hour to put his far-reaching plans into action. He planned to reconstitute the empire and started his reign by sweeping with an iron broom. He threw the numerous parasites at the court into the street in short order. He then purged the general public administration of undesirables. One measure followed the other. Not only were administration and army reorganized, but the old faith was to be restored. All at once the pagan temples reopened and the sacrifices were carried out. The emperor received a storm of applause in many places for this act, but he also saw with sadness that the mass of the people were indifferent. The Christians, as would be assumed, resisted bitterly. The emperor became uncertain and pressed his changes more hastily; even before one ordinance became completely known, let alone carried out, the next one followed. By intervening personally Julian attempted to carry the population along with him. But in vain! Instead of enthusiastic following he found, as a rule, surprise, even mockery.

The rule of Julian lasted only a few years. Constantius had died in the year 361, and while on an expedition against the Persians in June of 363, Julian was fatally wounded by the lance of a Persian rider. The Christians rejoiced. They saw Julian's early death as a sure sign of the judgment of God. The widespread rumor that a Christian had inflicted the deadly wound, however, is unfounded. Julian had attempted to turn back the wave of history, not because he was a blind fanatic, but because he overestimated the power of paganism. There were too few left who, like him, tried to live in the old faith. The age of the gods was really over, and nothing could revive it. When the persecution launched by Julian came, Athanasius had declared prophetically: "It is a little cloud, it will soon pass by." The further decline of paganism was inevitable; it was definitely a lost cause.

BASIL OF CAESAREA

An Old Question Resolved

In the first three centuries of church history Asia Minor played a leading role. When Constantine smoothed the way for the triumph of Christianity, Asia Minor had the largest percentage of Christians in its population. The other provinces followed far behind. Italy stood almost at the end of the line, although the Roman bishop had already extended his influence and control over the church in the West.

However, around 300 Asia Minor was no longer the focal point of the theological controversies. In the second century Asia Minor had still dominated theology. Almost all men who exercised a determining influence on the further development of theology and church either lived in Asia Minor or had come from there. This changed in the third century when Africa, with Tertullian and Cyprian, and Egypt, with Clement and Origen, assumed theological leadership. In the first half of the fourth century the prominence of Egypt could no longer be disputed: here Athanasius was at work, and here monasticism had its origin.

But in the fourth century the leadership of Egypt was successfully attacked by Constantinople as well as by Rome, and toward the end of the century Asia Minor once more arose to its old splendor before its final decline. The three "Great Cappadocians" were largely responsible for this resurgence: Basil the Great, as he is rightly called; his brother Gregory of Nyssa; and Gregory of Nazianzus, the friend of both.

The most important of the three was Basil. He was born around 330 of Christian parents in Caesarea of Cappadocia, his later place of activity. His mother was the daughter of a martyr. Besides Basil, two of his brothers were later consecrated as bishops, and several of his brothers and sisters devoted themselves to the monastic life. Yet Basil and his brother received their education completely in the spirit of late antiquity in which the scholarly education, even of Christians, was influenced by pagan literature and philosophy. First in his native city, then in Constantinople, and finally in Athens, Basil sat at the feet of the most famous teachers. It is interesting that he met Crown Prince Julian, who at the time was also a student. It was also during his student days that he met Gregory of Nazianzus and became his friend for life.

The striving for the ascetic life finally won out over Basil's love of knowledge. On his return to Asia Minor he was at first an orator because of his education; he later declined enticing offers in order to follow the example of his mother, brothers, and sisters who led an ascetic life on an estate belonging to the family. He now received baptism (this late date was not unusual in those days) and started on a journey to Syria, Palestine, and Egypt where he observed monasticism at its source, as had many others of his day. Filled with ascetic zeal, he returned home, gave all his possessions to the poor, and gathered about him those of like mind in a monastic fellowship.

But although the sympathies of Basil were always with the monastic life, he was repeatedly drawn into the ecclesiastical life and theological controversies of his time. The bishop of his native city was not capable of dealing with the difficult questions which disturbed the church at the time. The Arian controversies had not yet died; the battle lines on this issue, which had been rather clear at the beginning, had become so blurred and confusing that without sufficient theological training one could only too easily take the wrong turn. Between the true Arians who still enjoyed the support of the state and the strict *homoousians,* represented by the followers of Athanasius and the West, there were various intermediary groups. Some, with the court bishops at their head, were rather close to the Arians. They advocated a compromise theology, meeting the wishes of the state halfway and subsisting only because of the state's favor. Although the others could assert what Athanasius asserted so stubbornly, the form of his expression was not acceptable to them because it was subject to theological misunderstanding.

When Athanasius affirmed that the Father and the Son are of the same essence (Greek, *homoousios*), this seemed to them not to do sufficient justice to the difference between the Father and the Son which is attested to by Scripture. By no means did they want to subordinate the Son to the Father in essence and power, but they did want to designate their relationship in such a way that the proposition would remain theologically unobjectionable. Therefore they spoke of *homoiousios,* that is, similar in essence. Only in such a way, it seemed to them, could the full reality of divinity be preserved. Then came the question of the position of the Holy Spirit. It was Basil who found the way to a solution which combined the proper concern of Athanasius with the demands of the educated theologians. With his brother Gregory of Nyssa and his friend Gregory of Nazianzus, he found a solution to the Arian controversy. But he did not live to see the success of his efforts. He had been dead for two years when the Council of Constantinople met in 381 and brought an official end to the controversies.

The life of Basil was one of theological battles which had begun when he was elected bishop of Caesarea in 370 by a narrow margin. He had to defend himself against the state and against theological opponents as well. At times vested interests and personality differences were harder to fight than theological opponents and many times prevented agreement even when differing theological viewpoints had been reconciled. Basil's work as a church politician commands our respect. He labored untiringly for the church entrusted to him; his letters and his sermons bear witness to that. His sermons give an especially impressive picture. He spoke out against the shortcomings of his time with authority, exhorting, advising, and also fearlessly punishing. He was a true bishop! Despite his emphatically ascetic attitude, which to an extent caused his premature death, he was free of all narrowmindedness. His rules for monastic life, which emphasized the active love of neighbor, effectively limited the constant inclination of the monasticism of that time toward narrowness and spiritual egotism. And the fact that a large number of the writings of pagan antiquity have been preserved for us we owe to the monk-bishop Basil. It was his *Exhortation to the Youth About the Profitable Use of Pagan Literature* which preserved the treasures of the past without prejudice for the present and the future.

Both Gregorys, the one of Nyssa as well as the one of Nazianzus, were also bishops. For a time Gregory of Nazianzus was patriarch of Constantinople. But neither of them approached the stature of Basil. This is why Gregory of Nazianzus administered the bishop's office in Constantinople for only a short time. He did not feel equal to the ecclesio-political battles which raged so heatedly there, and so he voluntarily resigned. In the conflict between the demands of ecclesiastical office and the love of ascetic withdrawal and scholarly work, the inclination to the latter won each time, just as with Gregory of Nyssa.

Yet the significance of these men for the church is not small. For instance, Gregory of Nazianzus received the honorary title "the Theologian" for the addresses which he delivered in Constantinople. Both Gregory of Nyssa with his *Great Catechesis* and his writings about his sister Macrina, and Gregory of Nazianzus with his sermons, orations, and poetry, exercised a strong influence over the years that followed. Their greatest achievement was showing the church a way to put aside the age-old Arian controversies. They had found a solution of one of the basic questions of Christianity, and to this day no one has gone beyond their answer.

DAMASUS OF ROME

An Early Pope

Throughout this book frequent mention has been made of the Roman church and its bishops. We have spoken of the origin of the Christian congregation in Rome, of Clement, of Calixtus and Hippolytus, of Cornelius, of Stephen I, of Dionysius, and of Liberius. But with the exception of Clement and Calixtus, our mention of the bishop of Rome has always been made when treating other personalities. Some bishops have been taken into consideration without mentioning their names. Was that intentional? Have we slighted the Roman bishops or popes (a title which they bore at first along with other bishops, and not until later with the claim of exclusiveness)? No, no partiality was involved.

Of the many bishops who reigned in Rome in the almost four centuries which have been covered up to this point, none who was of essential significance for the total development of the church has been overlooked. The fact of the matter is that in the early period Rome did not have that significance for the history of the church which we often ascribe to her because we wrongly project the conditions of later centuries onto the early period. By the Middle Ages things had changed; by then Rome had become the center of Western Christianity. But in the earlier centuries Christianity had numerous centers, and other bishops than those of Rome exercised significant influence over the development of theology and the church. None of the popes in the earlier centuries really had the stature of a hero or a saint. The first great bishop of Rome, Leo I (who will be treated in a separate chapter), lived in the middle of the fifth century. But he is alone in his prominence. Perhaps Innocent I could be mentioned along with him. But Innocent's claim to fame fades beside the achievements of his contemporary, Augustine! Soon after the death of Leo I the popes were relegated to a very minor role. Thirty years later we see them in depressing dependence, first on the rulers of the Ostrogoths and later on the Byzantine emperors. This degraded condition of the papacy sadly contrasted with its sweeping claims and lasted for one hundred years. Not until Gregory I (590-604) did the papacy rise from its weakness, only to sink into it again soon after him.

This is how things really were. For the doubter the proof can be quickly furnished. Later on we will speak further of the popes of the period of the Ostrogoths and the Byzantine period. But for the present let us consider just the fourth century. The most significant of the eleven popes of this period was Damasus. To begin with, Damasus was a man with theological interests. He did some writing and had a scholarly relationship with Jerome. Naturally it is easy to look mockingly at his letters to Jerome in which he sought theological instruction, for there are a number of points which invite such treatment. But to do this would be unjustified, for a bishop, especially of that time, cannot be measured by the same standards as a professor of theology.

The fact that under Damasus the great work of the Vulgate Bible was begun by Jerome should cause us not to dismiss Damasus' scholarship too easily. This work was the creation of a unified translation of the Latin Bible which up to this time was circulated in various editions. For a Roman bishop of his time, he was interested in scholarly things to a striking degree. He instigated the construction of a new building for the papal archives. He repaired the neglected tombs and memorials to the apostles, bishops, and martyrs and decorated them with marble plaques on which their contributions and achievements were commemorated by verses of his own composition.

However, one cannot go so far as to assert that Damasus did all this purely out of scholarly interest and out of a delight in history. Rather completely different intentions also played a role, perhaps a decisive role. Well-ordered archives from which one can take whatever material is needed have been useful weapons in ecclesiastical power struggles in every age for those who know how to use them. Either good archives or an extraordinarily accurate memory were necessary to oversee and understand the confusion of the entire Arian controversy, especially during the final stage when Damasus was pope. Besides, the position of Rome needed to be fortified against the insubordination of the Orientals, and for that, recalling the glorious early history of the Roman church was the best weapon. It is on this basis that Damasus' concern for the tombs of Christian leaders and martyrs can be explained. Of course, Damasus' own vanity played a role in his concern for these burial places, for the plaques with which they were marked bore verses composed by him. But the most decisive concern of Damasus was ecclesio-political. Everything he did aimed at furthering the fame and influence of the "apostolic see."

This term was coined and applied to Rome by Damasus and has been used in Rome ever since. Constantinople asserted its prestige with considerable effort, and successfully claimed the second place of honor in the ecclesiastical list of rank on the basis of being the new Rome, that is, the new capital of the world. If this assertion of Constantinople was to be challenged and if that see was to be prevented from advancing its goals even further, then the most effective weapon for Rome was to point to its double apostolic beginnings. Constantinople had been founded in the recent past and any attempt to claim that the congregation there had been founded by the apostles was without any kind of support, not even by the boldest ecclesiastical "source research." Nor did Constantinople have as many martyrs as Rome. This was probably the principal motive behind Damasus' concern for the Roman ecclesiastical past. Damasus was a strong-willed man who made everything serve the goal he had in view, and then he marched toward that goal with iron determination, kicking every obstacle out of the way.

Basil of Caesarea spoke quite bitterly about Damasus. Ironically he called him a man who "exaltedly removed from the earth, is enthroned so high that the voices which speak the truth from below are unable to get through to him." This was in reference to the attitude of Damasus toward Basil's efforts to find a solution for the problems which impeded the conclusion of the Arian controversies. In this matter Damasus held himself aloof from all approaches by the East. He did not want to meet the bishops of the Orient on the level of equality. And whoever tried to approach him as an equal, as Basil rightfully did, could not hope to be heard. Moreover, Damasus did not want to negotiate; he wanted to see his decisions accepted by the East without contradiction. He maintained the old relationships to Alexandria because the Egyptian bishop was the confidant of Rome, and therefore he deserved a preeminent position in the East. If one did not recognize this and went one's own way, as the East did, then one could not hope for support from Rome.

The so-called Three Emperor Edict of 380 which decreed that all Christianity "should live in the faith which the apostle Peter handed down to the Romans . . . the faith which the Pontifex Damasus and Peter of Alexandria, the bishop of apostolic holiness, confess," was entirely to the liking of Damasus. On the other hand, he was incensed by the decisions of the imperial Council of Constantinople of 381, ratified by the emperor, which led the controversial questions of doctrine to an independent solution without the participation of Rome and which also restricted every bishop to a certain area (for example, the Alexandrian to Egypt) and thus hindered rather than furthered Rome's attempt to assert its supremacy over the other bishoprics (until now it was still a matter of Rome's priority rather than supremacy). Damasus continued on his way without regard to this provision. He had a Roman synod immediately after 381 speak of the "primacy of the Roman church,"

not of Peter as was done until then, and he demanded for Alexandria the second rank in Christianity, as if the Council of Constantinople in 381 had never happened. He asserted that Alexandria
was founded in the name of the apostle Peter by his disciple Mark.

We may be impressed by this boldness, but can we agree with
such tactics? The price that Rome paid for the stubbornness of
Damasus was growing estrangement from the East and constantly
increasing bitterness. Estrangement and bitterness were to have
painful consequences later on, but they certainly did not impress
Damasus, who was accustomed to taking all obstacles in stride.

How had Damasus come to his office? The reports about this
are instructive. Pope Liberius died on September 24, 366. Immediately the Roman clergy split into two parties. The smaller one
elected the deacon Ursinus, the larger one, the deacon Damasus
as successor to the late pope. The majority group was still assembled when the message arrived that Ursinus had already been made
bishop and had received consecration. What was to be done? A
crowd armed with sticks (where did the crowd come from?)
immediately stormed toward the church in which the followers of
Ursinus were assembled, and attacked them (who gave the word?).
The battle lasted for three days while Damasus remained in hiding
with a bodyguard in the Lateran. Finally Ursinus was banned from
Rome and Damasus could be consecrated bishop.

The competitor had been removed, but he still had supporters
among the Roman clergy. They, too, were to be driven from the
city, but instead their followers flocked together and took them
to safety in the church of Liberius. Now, four weeks after the
election of Damasus, a formal battle for the possession of this
church ensued. The troops of Damasus advanced, this time armed
not only with sticks but with hatchets and swords. Some climbed
on the roof of the church and tore off tiles which they dropped on
their opponents, who were assembled in the house of God. Others
broke down the doors, started a fire, and finally took the church by
storm. According to some reports the followers of Ursinus counted
one hundred thirty-seven dead, whereas the followers of Damasus

suffered not a single fatality. This does not include the number of those who died later from the injuries sustained.

This was how Damasus ascended the bishop's throne and how he secured his reign. It is to be understood that the reported cruelties were not the only crimes perpetrated even if they were the worst. For years worshipping assemblies of the followers of Ursinus were interrupted, and priests were dragged before the court. No one would care to assert that Damasus did not know of these procedures or that he was not involved in them. And the fact that violent acts occurred elsewhere cannot serve as an excuse.

Still another dark shadow falls across Damasus. In the year 371 a very unusual thing took place: Damasus was charged at court with criminal acts. The judge accepted the charge, and a trial was held even though Damasus certainly enjoyed the favor of the state. The charges, then, must have been quite serious, although it can no longer be determined definitely what they were, for the matter was suppressed. In any case, it looked bad for Damasus at the time. A number of the clergy had been questioned, even under torture, when Damasus succeeded in bringing the case before the emperor, who acquitted him.

One source speaks of the charge of adultery. The fact that Damasus evidently stood in a close connection with various groups of noble and rich women gives some plausibility to this charge. Slanderous and mocking rumors circulated because of this; the state even considered it necessary to issue a special edict to prevent legacy hunting by clergy in these circles. Or perhaps it was a charge of murder or inducement to murder, for Damasus was already sixty years old when he assumed the bishop's throne and he should have been beyond temptation by the opposite sex. The events following the election of Damasus certainly offered sufficient grounds for indictment, but it seems doubtful that a trial would have been instituted on this basis. In any case, Damasus considered it necessary, seven years later, to justify himself in detail before an Italian synod. The synod declared the accusations as slanderous, but we still do not know what it was all about.

One might wonder why Damasus waited such a long time to justify himself before the church. Did he have to let some time pass until the excitement subsided? Or did traces have to be wiped out? Let us avoid further speculation and stop here. For what is reported probably is sufficient. The clear truth is that the Roman bishops of the first centuries are not very promising candidates for the titles of heroes and saints. Also they were definitely not the dominant figures of their time. Damasus was far surpassed in the East by Basil and in the West by Ambrose, the bishop of nearby Milan. Neither he nor any other pope of the fourth century can be compared with them.

THEODOSIUS THE GREAT

Not in a Vacuum

At the beginning of the fourth century Constantine had united the empire by force. Step by step he had subjected first the West and then the East to his rule. At his death, rule of the empire was divided among his three sons. But before long Constantius reunited that which had been divided, although there were extensive losses in the East and in the West, for he suffered some serious defeats at the hands of both the Persians and the Germans. Julian's rule brought about some improvement of the situation, but his reign was too brief. His successor, Jovian, was not the man to carry on what Julian had begun. Furthermore, Jovian's reign lasted only eight months.

Therefore, when the two brothers, Valentinian I and Valens, were made emperors by the military, the imperial power was again divided, as had been the case before Constantine and under his sons. The only difference was that the imperial power had decreased. The Persians had become more and more enterprising, and the Germans, who until now had threatened only the Rhine border, began to attack the empire from the Danube. The migrations had begun, and the flood set in motion by the Huns raged higher and higher, first against the tottering outposts, and soon against the heartland of the Roman Empire. Valens fell in battle against the Goths. The situation was stabilized only because Gratian, who in 375 at the age of sixteen had succeeded his father Valentinian I, turned the rule in the East over to Theodosius, who had more military experience. Theodosius halted the advances of the Germans. Nevertheless, the situation of the empire still remained rather unstable. The power crisis had only shifted.

A few years after Gratian had gained the energetic support of Theodosius, his rule was challenged by one of his generals, Maximus. Under Maximus' leadership, Britain and Gaul rebelled against Gratian. Gratian tried in vain to suppress the rebellion, but his troops deserted him. He was killed, and now the empire had three rulers. Beside Theodosius in the East and Maximus in the extreme West there was still the twelve-year-old Valentinian II, who so far had stood completely in the shadow of his brother Gratian. This condition continued for not quite five years. Then Maximus attempted to overthrow Valentinian, who had maintained his position only by the support of German generals. Maximus invaded Italy and forced Valentinian to flee. Valentinian found refuge with Theodosius, who in the meantime had become Valentinian's brother-in-law.

Even after Maximus had been defeated by Theodosius, Valentinian was not able to return as the ruler. He spent his last years in Gaul, a ruler in name only, closely guarded by Arbogast the Frank. Scholars disagree whether Valentinian II was killed by Arbogast or whether he committed suicide in despair. In any case, a few months after Valentinian's death, Arbogast chose a successor in the person of Eugenius, thus beginning the practice whereby German generals named figurehead emperors whom they controlled. Eugenius had penetrated into Italy and was aiming at winning control of the whole empire when Theodosius defeated his army.

Finally the empire had been united under one strong hand. But only a few more months were granted to the victor. In September of 394 the decisive battle against Eugenius had been fought; in January of 395 Theodosius died. Again the empire was divided, this time between the two sons of the deceased, Arcadius and Honorius. Arcadius received the East, his brother the West. Arcadius neglected, as had Valens before, one of the most important considerations: establishing a mutual understanding with the Germans who had settled in the area of the Danube. Because Arcadius did not continue to pay them the sums agreed upon, the Visigoths, under the leadership of Alaric, swept over the empire, and they were only defeated with the aid of troops supplied by the Western half of the empire.

The East was saved because Arcadius, by diplomacy, had succeeded in directing the Visigoths against the Western Empire (which had just sent its armies to his defense!). Here the German Stilicho, who played a decisive role as the marshal of the Western Empire, was able at first to build a protective wall which kept the Goths from penetrating westward. But in 408 Honorius had him murdered, and now there was no bulwark. Alaric the Goth marched against Rome three times, and it was finally forced to surrender in August 410 and was thoroughly sacked. Already Vandals, Swabians, and Alemanni had invaded Spain; Gaul was lost to the Germans; Britain was practically given up.

Although Honorius was successful in reconquering Gaul and a part of Spain as well, this conquest was possible only because he was able to play Germans off against Germans. These successes were only apparent and transitory, however. For while Honorius was still living the empire of the Visigoths in Spain and Southern Gaul made itself independent of Rome and existed for almost three hundred years until it succumbed to the attack of the Arabs. The Vandals in 429, a few years after the death of Honorius, went on to Africa where they solidly established their rule for a century.

This is a brief picture of the political situation in the Roman Empire during the fourth century. Even though we are primarily interested in the history of the church we must give some attention to secular events because they are of great importance for the understanding of the history of Christianity in the waning fourth century. Only by paying attention to the political fluctuations can one understand the zigzag course which church politics steered on many issues. For example, until the death of his brother Constans, Constantius was forced to curb his endeavors on behalf of Arianism. However, when he became sole ruler he soon brought the West under his ecclesiastical dictatorship and continued to steer a course away from Nicaea's decision on the question of Arianism.

Under the sons of Constantine paganism was restricted; on the accession of Julian it received a new impetus. The emperors after Julian wanted to continue the Christian course of the sons of Constantine. But as long as they were not secure in the saddle they were forced to take into consideration the pagan upper class. This class took advantage of the weakness of the emperors and made several attempts to restore paganism to its previous position. The emperors' hostility toward paganism increased as their rule solidified, while the usurpers on their part favored paganism because they hoped to attract supporters by such tactics. Thus, for example, Eugenius at first cultivated the friendship of Ambrose and with it a relationship to the Catholic church. But when he was not successful he made himself the spokesman for a group favoring pagan restoration. Therefore the battle between Eugenius and Theodosius became at the same time a religious war.

On the other hand the emperors were sometimes inclined to favor the Arians. If they were secure in their power, they would follow their Arian inclination, as did Valens, for example. If the position of the emperors was difficult, they curbed their religious policy as soon as serious opposition developed. This is what happened with Valentinian II who, at the instigation of his mother Justina, had attempted on several occasions to provide room for Arianism at least in his city of residence, Milan. He had to submit to Ambrose, the spokesman and leader of the orthodox Catholic majority of the population, in order not to endanger his position. Because he did not submit as quickly and as fully as he might have, his rival Maximus won an increase in popularity. All that Valentinian won were the reproaches of Theodosius, with whom he then was forced to seek refuge.

It is a fact that church history and secular history are closely bound together, and one cannot concern oneself with the history of Christianity without at the same time keeping one's eye on the history of nations and the general development of politics and culture. The history of the church does not develop in a vacuum but among people and through people, often even indirectly through people who have and desire to have nothing at all to do with the church and with Christianity. Despite this, what they do is guided by the hidden hand of God. However, we cannot claim certainty about God's detailed willing and acting. We must stay with the events before our eyes and attempt to determine what factors influence them. The political considerations which, in the past as well as in the present, can be recognized only by close scrutiny are certainly among the most important and influential factors.

AMBROSE OF MILAN

An Impartial Bishop

"Make me bishop of the city of Rome, and I will become a Christian at once," the city prefect of Rome, one of the noblest and richest men of the city, is reported to have said to Bishop Damasus. The remark was made in jest, but it points to a definite reality. At the end of the fourth century the bishops of the major cities occupied a position which paralleled that of high ranking secular lords in influence and splendor, if indeed it did not far exceed that position. "When they have achieved this (the Roman bishop's office, although the situation in other cities is the same), they are completely secure for the future: Through the donations of the ladies they become rich, ride around in coaches, dress in fine clothes, and hold such immoderate banquets that their dinners surpass the royal tables," wrote Ammianus Marcellinus in a bitter reflection on the time of Damasus. Marcellinus was a pagan, but he was unfortunately absolutely right, as Jerome confirms in his reports about the life of the Roman clergy.

Eight years after the tumults in Rome which attended the election of Damasus as bishop of that city, the bishop of Milan died. There was the possibility of unrest in connection with the election of a successor. The controversies of the Arian battle still played a part. In order to quiet the controversies, the widely beloved governor of the province, Ambrose, entered the church in which the opposing parties were gathered. When the controversy quieted down, Ambrose, instead of one of the original candidates, was elected bishop—by acclamation. He was a layman, not even baptized as yet. But he accepted the office. Baptism was speedily administered, and a short time later the consecration of the new bishop took place.

Is this a case which might remind us of what was just reported about Rome? Indeed Milan was not Rome, but next to Rome it was the most important city of Italy as far as religious and political matters were concerned. For a long time the bishop of Milan had been an annoying rival to Rome. Did Ambrose use the occasion offered to him or perhaps even desired by him in order to transfer from public office into an ecclesiastical career from which he could expect more honor, success, and riches for himself? No, this suspicion is unjustified. For one thing, Ambrose belonged to one of the foremost families of the empire and his position as the governor of two provinces, a position to which he had attained by his middle thirties, guaranteed that he had every prospect of advancing far in public service. Furthermore, he attempted to withdraw from the office offered to him. If he accepted the bishop's post despite his misgivings, it was because he took his Christianity seriously. His parents were Christians and were close to the church. His sister had taken the vow of chastity in her youth, and when Ambrose was elected bishop his brother entered ecclesiastical service at the same time as his aide. The fact that Ambrose himself was not yet baptized was not unusual. Even Emperor Constantius was not baptized until he lay on his deathbed. Ambrose was one of those bishops of whom Ammianus Marcellinus spoke with respect in spite of his dislike of the Roman Catholic church because, as he said, their attitude "recommends them to the deity and his true worshippers as pure men worthy of respect."

For the first time a man of such eminent position undertook the bishop's office in the West, an event which made a widespread and lasting impression. Quite angrily the successor of Damasus in Rome spoke of the fact that it was unseemly for some one who had never held a church office to be elected presbyter. "He who has not yet learned anything, is already forced to teach. Can no one suitable be found among the clergy, either among the deacons or among others who would be worthy of the presbyter's office? Must a layman be elected, to shame the church?" Cautiously he did not mention the bishop's office, but it is quite clear whom he meant—Ambrose. Indeed, Ambrose gave the Roman bishop reason for being apprehensive: there could be no doubt that at that time Ambrose was the real pope of the West.

A few years after the accession of Ambrose, Emperor Valentinian I died. The government then passed into the hands of his sixteen-year-old son Gratian. Ambrose became Gratian's spiritual mentor; he instructed him in regard to the complicated questions of the Arian controversy, which had not yet come to an end, and also exercised a practical influence on his general policies. At that time Gratian renounced the title of *Pontifex Maximus,* pagan chief priest, which the emperors had borne from ancient times. In connection with this the altar of Victoria, that symbol of the Roman spirit, set up under Augustus, was removed from the hall of the Senate. Both of these actions dealt severe blows to paganism, for this also meant the cessation of contributions from the public treasury to the various pagan fellowships which were greatly dependent on them, whereas the Christian church was still able, despite all the donations of the emperors, to maintain its financial independence.

The removal of the pagan symbol of Victoria from the Senate challenged the members of the Senate, the majority of whom still practiced paganism. Once before the statue had been touched —by Emperor Constantine. But it was missing from its customary place only a few years, for Julian had quickly restored it, and during the next twenty years it adorned the Senate. But the attempt of the Senate to have Gratian revoke his edict was to no avail. Its delegates were not even able to get an audience with him: Ambrose was wise enough to prevent it!

When Gratian died a violent death and twelve-year-old Valentinian II became the real ruler, the influence of Ambrose increased. He even became the representative of the political interests of the young ruler, a task for which he was well equipped. But the pagan upper class had not yet given up hope of regaining its former rights. The city prefect of Rome, Symmachus, a highly educated and a well-known man, appeared before the emperor and petitioned him to restore the Victoria to the Senate (that is, to restore to the pagan cults their old financial rights). The statue was the symbol of the rule of Rome, which had become great and powerful under the old faith, he declared. Equal rights and tolerance—that was the demand of Symmachus, nothing more.

The emperor and his advisers were evidently inclined to grant the request so effectively presented. Then Ambrose intervened. He wrote a letter to the ruler and adjured him not to give in to the demand of Symmachus. He openly threatened his emperor with excommunication. What bishop up to that time would have dared to go so far! Ambrose was successful: both the emperor and the council declined the petition of Symmachus. For the second time the maneuver of the old faith had been blocked.

A year later a new conflict arose. The mother of the emperor, Justina, requested that a church be set aside outside the gates of Milan in which special services could be held for her entourage and the German bodyguard of the emperor. There would have been no argument against this; the city had enough churches, why should not one be made available to the court? But the bodyguard consisted of Arians, and Justina had often enough given expression to her dissatisfaction at the decisions of Nicaea and the *homoousios*. Therefore, Ambrose declined her request outright. His life's work was dedicated to the solidification and spread of the pure faith. It was impossible for him, who had successfully repressed Arianism in the empire, to fulfill the imperial wish.

After some squabbling, Justina, the mother of the emperor and widow of the previous ruler, had the church confiscated. When the people rebelled, the court sought to crush resistance by many arrests and by high fines. In vain! Another attempt to take possession of a church, this time within the city, also failed. An

edict of banishment was issued against Ambrose, who declared
he would not obey it. A religious disputation was to decide the
controversial questions, but Ambrose refused to participate. Night
and day the believers gathered in the church threatened with confiscation, singing hymns (at the time Ambrose composed his first
hymns) and listening to the sermons which openly encouraged
them to resist. When Ambrose finally threatened to excommuni-
cate the soldiers who had surrounded the church, they left their
posts in droves and went over to the congregation. Finally the
emperor yielded. Valentinian even had to accept the admoni-
tions of his officers to participate in the service of Ambrose as a
sign of reconciliation. "You would turn me over to him in bonds
if Ambrose commanded you," he declared angrily.

When Valentinian later fled before the approaching Maximus
to take refuge with Theodosius, and the latter, after the defeat
of Maximus, had assumed the rule over the West as well, Ambrose
boldly represented the demands of the church, even before this
much more powerful emperor. At the occasion of the restoration
of the synagogue of Callinicum, we see Ambrose as the pro-
ponent of a doubtful cause. Yet we have to admire his courageous
stand. In the border city of Callinicum, which was in the East of
the empire, the Christians had set fire to the Jewish house of
worship, probably at the instigation of their bishop. Theodosius
gave orders that the arsonists should be punished and that the
bishop should have the synagogue restored. A letter of protest
from Ambrose was only half-successful. He then addressed the
emperor in his next sermon and would not go to the altar to
offer the sacrifice of the mass until Theodosius had promised not
only to rescind the punishment but also to cease investigation
of the incident.

Theodosius, as had the emperors before him, after taking over
the government of the Western Empire, had several times shown
himself friendly toward paganism. That was necessary in order
not to alienate the upper classes. When the Senate came to him
with the request to reinstate financial support of the pagan cults,
the emperor seemed inclined to grant it. No doubt this would

have brought him much goodwill. But Ambrose heard about it, and for the third time he was successful in blocking the efforts of the pagan aristocracy. He wrote to the emperor and held himself aloof from the court for a few days (when he did not get a speedy positive answer), until Theodosius, as Gratian and Valentinian before him, yielded to his wishes.

Ambrose is most impressive and most likable after the events of Thessalonica. Here a popular rebellion had ensued during which the supreme commander of the imperial troops was killed. Theodosius, in reprisal, began a blood bath among the people who had been gathered together in the circus. There many hundreds of completely innocent persons lost their lives. The order for this mass murder had been given by Theodosius in a fit of rage. When he regained his senses the horrible deed had already been done. The letter which Ambrose now addressed to the emperor was written by him personally and was meant only for the eyes of the emperor: no angel or archangel could absolve him from this deed. Only the Lord himself could pardon him and then only if the emperor were truly penitent. If the emperor refused this judgment, Ambrose would not be able to perform the sacrifice of the mass in his presence. Thus Ambrose threatened him with excommunication. He had done this before to Valentinian II, in contrast to whom Theodosius was not a young man but a powerful ruler of the world. Yet even he was forced to bow before Ambrose. Stripped of the insignia of his imperial position he appeared in the church and confessed his guilt before the congregation. Not until eight months later did Ambrose admit him again to communion.

One might think that Ambrose already had asserted the claims of the papacy during the high Middle Ages and that this was an event which paralleled the penitential appearance of Henry IV at Canossa, but this is not so. Ambrose was far removed from asserting an ecclesiastical claim to temporal power and perhaps intending to force the empire to submit to the church. His concern regarding the event which took place in Milan in 390 was completely different. Here Christianity was taken completely seriously. The same behavior that is demanded of every Christian is demanded even of the ruler of the world. On breaking the commandments he also fell under the threats of punishment of the gospel. Only if he submitted—not to the bishop or to the church, but to God—could he receive absolution. Ambrose did not think of attacking the governmental power or the authority of the emperor. He simply dared to execute the duties of his office without partiality.

Naturally the papacy of later times did not fail to appeal to the actions of Ambrose. But actually Ambrose was anything but a promoter of the Roman claims. First, he considered the church in general not as a power factor or an institution parallel to the state, but as a purely spiritual communion. Second, in his ecclesiastical politics, Ambrose took notice of the existence of the bishop in Rome only to such an extent as seemed absolutely necessary. Furthermore, he made his decisions without, and if necessary even against, Rome, completely according to his judgment and the necessities of his upper Italian church province.

Under Ambrose, the Milan bishop's see was a serious contender against the Roman see. Yet it must be noted that Ambrose, without wanting to do so, actually strengthened the power of the Catholic church and immensely advanced its development to the form which prevailed in the Middle Ages. For not the gospel but the church was the center of his thinking, even if his conception of the church differed from that of medieval Catholicism. Faith was consent to the teaching of the church; without this, it has no firm standing. The church mediates salvation: it is the embodiment of Christianity; it is important that the church is right.

No doubt Ambrose was a scriptural theologian. He was familiar with the Bible in a most impressive way; throughout his writings he appeals to it. The significance of his writings, however, is secondary to that of his personality and his practical work; they were part and parcel of his activity of leading the church. And yet it was not Scripture that ruled the life and work of Ambrose, but the thought of the church. Scripture was effective for him and according to him only through the church and for the church.

AUGUSTINE

"Pick It Up, Read It"

Ambrose was consecrated bishop of Milan on December 6, 373; Augustine was called to be a teacher of rhetoric at Milan at the beginning of the year 384. Ambrose was born between 333 and 340 and died in 397; Augustine was born in 354 and died in 430. The life span of these two men overlapped; they were contemporaries who shared close personal ties. Augustine turned to Christianity during his stay at Milan. Ambrose was not just the one by whom Augustine was baptized at Easter 387; he also played a considerable part in Augustine's decision to become a Christian, although the conversion itself was influenced by other factors of which we shall speak later.

The Western church under Ambrose and Augustine reached a height unparalleled before or since. Ambrose was a bishop whose significance and effectiveness made everything before him seem pallid. He surpassed not only all the popes of the early period (with the exception of Leo I and Gregory I who belong to the middle of the fifth century and to the beginning of the seventh century respectively), but also all Western church leaders who are known to us. Cyprian, for instance, is by far his inferior in personal influence as well as in his theological contributions. Ambrose, in turn, is far surpassed by Augustine, who was also a bishop.

Augustine was consecrated in 395, first as an associate bishop along with Valerius at Hippo in Northern Africa; soon he took over the leadership of the diocese by himself. As a bishop he exerted an influence over all of Northern Africa during the Donatist controversy, and far beyond his home province in the Pelagian controversy. With Ambrose the emphasis lay on the practical side of the bishop's office, the theological side had to take second place. With Augustine the situation was reversed. Augustine was the theologian of the West in the early church; his significance for the West corresponded to that of Origen for the East.

Let us look back for a moment. We have met Irenaeus, Tertullian, Hippolytus, Novatian, Cyprian, and Ambrose. No doubt Tertullian had a decisive effect on the theological development of the West, but this happened, so to speak, on the edge of things, not within the context of a developed system. Cyprian and Ambrose were equals: for both of them theological activity ensued from the necessities of their office and their time. That would leave Irenaeus, Hippolytus, Novatian, and, if you wish, Hilary of Poitiers, who in the middle of the fourth century became involved in the Arian controversy. Indeed Hilary, for example, was one of the few Westerners who really understood the questions with which the East was concerned in this controversy, but actually he only repeated the thought of the Eastern theologians; he did not contribute to a solution.

The importance of Irenaeus should not be minimized, but neither he nor Hippolytus nor Novatian can be fairly compared to Augustine. It can be said that Augustine was not only *the* theologian of the West in the early period of the church, he was also *the* church father, almost the father of the Catholic church as such, as far as such a statement is at all possible.

Tertullian, whom the church was prevented from recognizing because of his conversion to Montanism, had a similar importance for the third and fourth century. What would the church of the West have done without the theological assertions of Tertullian in the Arian and the Christological controversies? But from the time of Augustine on, Tertullian's significance waned. Augustine built on the foundation laid by Tertullian in such a way that one saw only the proud doctrinal building of Augustine, even though the Catholic church did not occupy all the rooms in Augustine's edifice and, in fact, expanded and rebuilt it so much during the course of the centuries that many times only very little of Augustine's original structure could be recognized.

Not only for the Catholic church has Augustine been of significance. Augustine's influence and importance was such that Luther characterized his study of Augustine as a decisive factor in gaining his reformation insight! Indeed, one can orient the development of church history around three focal points: Paul, Augustine, and Luther. Augustine discovered Paul anew, although some before him—for example, Marius Victorinus, the so-called Ambrosiaster, and Tyconius—had made advances in this direction. Indeed, Augustine discovered the most decisive part of Paul; without Paul, Augustine's doctrine of the sinfulness of mankind and of the grace of God, which alone can save, would be unthinkable. Over a thousand years later Luther made the same discovery and, by reading Paul, became certain of justification by faith.

But one must be careful not to see Augustine and Luther as one even though Luther often enough appealed to Augustine as his chief witness. Luther read Augustine with his own eyes and interpreted him as more of an evangelical than he really was. Take, for example, Augustine's doctrine of the church. According to him, faith is not possible without authority, for authority is the presupposition for faith. Indeed, the goal is knowledge, but faith in that which the church teaches (that is, obedience), precedes knowledge: "I would not believe the gospel if the authority of the Catholic church did not move me to do so"!

According to Augustine the church has four marks: unity, universality, holiness, and agreement with tradition. Love can exist only in unity; he who separates himself from the (Catholic) church and breaks the unity does not love. Such a person can achieve much, but he will not achieve salvation. He who stands outside the (Catholic) church also has the gospel and the sacraments, but not to his profit; they do not work salvation for him. The truth of the church is proved by the fact that it is everywhere in the world, and this church tradition is valid even if it is not grounded in the Scriptures. If the church teaches something, we may assume that the apostles already taught the same thing, even when the Scriptures do not speak about it. To be sure, there are unworthy members in the church on earth, yet the church is without error. In the church salvation is guaranteed, and it can be gained only by belonging to the church. All this is in accord with Catholic thinking; we should not overlook these elements and make too much of an evangelical out of Augustine. Indeed, Augustine's doctrine of the church as just described is not the whole Augustine, and there are even traits in his doctrine of the church which point beyond this line of thinking. But it must not be forgotten that this attitude also belongs to him.

Probably the best known of all of Augustine's writings is his *Confessions,* in which he tells the story of his life. He was born on November 13, 354, at Thagaste in North African Numidia. His parents belonged to the middle class and made every effort to provide their son with as good an education as possible in order to guarantee him a good position in life. This striving for fame, honor, riches, and for a marriage that would enhance his social standing filled the heart of Augustine more than anything else. When he was still young his father, Patricius, who was not a Christian at Augustine's birth, was moved by his wife to become a Christian. But this conversion had no special significance.

If Augustine's youth was completely imbued with Christianity, then it is to the credit of his mother Monica. Her Christianity was tainted with a certain narrowness and some superstition. She was typical of the aspiring middle class of the small town of Thagaste. As a child Augustine became a catechumen, an applicant for baptism. During a severe illness he pleaded with his mother to let him be baptized. (This was characteristic of the time; Augustine's father was baptized only shortly before his death.) Because the illness soon abated, nothing came of his request.

In Thagaste Augustine was unable to receive a higher education. Therefore he was sent to study in Madaura, which called for great sacrifice on the part of his parents. When he returned, Augustine could not immediately pursue yet higher studies because his parents were unable to finance them. After the death of Augustine's father, a wealthy inhabitant of Thagaste gave Augustine the necessary means for continuing his education. In Carthage, where Augustine studied rhetoric (that is, in modern terms, the liberal arts), the temptations of the city devoured the hot-blooded youth. At least Augustine portrayed it in this way later on in his *Confessions,* where he never tired of painting the corruption of his youth as black as possible.

But on close examination one realizes that Augustine exaggerated greatly. He joined in student pranks, but without taking part in those which went beyond the limits of responsibility. He had a concubine, who bore him a son. But in those days concubinage was considered as a marriage of lower rank and was not completely condemned, not even by the church. In fact, in those early years in Carthage he took the first step on the way which would lead later to his conversion. A writing of Cicero, *Hortensius,* came into his hand. "Now it was this book which quite definitely changed my whole attitude and turned my prayers toward thee, O Lord, and gave me new hope and new desires. Suddenly every vain hope became worthless to me, and with an incredible warmth of heart I yearned for an immortality of wisdom and began now to arise that I might return to thee."

Augustine at the time was nineteen years of age. He read again and again this writing of Cicero and sought to put his intention of turning toward God into action right away by applying himself to the study of the Bible. But having just come from the elegant language of this Roman author, who lived shortly before the birth of Christ, and from his philosophical training, the Scriptures seemed to him unpolished in language, simple in content, even unintelligent. Dissatisfied, he came under the influence of the teaching of the Manicheans, who claimed that theirs was a true Christianity, purified of all its dross.

Manicheism was at the time strongly opposed by the church and was looked upon as one of the arch-heresies, and Augustine later regretted his affiliation with it; but at the time it offered him, coming as he did from the study of philosophy, something to think about in his search for truth. Mani, the founder of this movement, was born in 215 or 216 to a princely Persian family and was crucified around 275. He combined Gnostic Christianity and Eastern wisdom and religion. Augustine belonged to this fellowship for nine years, uniquely attracted to and repelled by it at the same time. Although he gained a number of adherents for it, among them his best friend, whose later return to the church made a deep impression on him, Augustine did not feel that his striving for knowledge was completely satisfied by Manicheism. He had centered his whole hope on meeting Faustus, one of the leading Manicheans. His disappointment was very great when Faustus was unable to answer satisfactorily Augustine's questions.

The young seeker then turned to a philosophical group which doubted everything and held that it is impossible for man to attain to the full truth. He had sought truth but had not found it; in the future he would devote himself to a doctrine only if he found it absolutely true and solidly founded against all doubt. Thus he vacillated among the Christian heritage of his youth, the remainder of Manichean thought, and the arguments of sceptical philosophy as he pursued his profession as a teacher of rhetoric in Thagaste, Carthage, Rome, and Milan.

It was in Milan that he came into a close association with Ambrose. No doubt professional curiosity was a factor in leading him to the celebrated preacher; Ambrose was a successful rhetorician, and rhetoric was the subject that Augustine taught. This professional relationship with Ambrose soon became a personal one. His sermons gripped Augustine. Through them many of his objections to the Old Testament, which was rejected by the

Manicheans as well as by Gnosticism, were overcome. Ambrose taught him to interpret the Old Testament allegorically.

Nevertheless, Augustine still did not find peace in his struggles. It was the question of God and of the origin of evil which perpetuated his unrest. In addition, worldly concerns still held him fast. As a teacher of eloquence he was forced to face the necessity of earning a living and to seek sponsors who could acquire a lucrative position for him, possibly in government service. His mother, who was with him in Milan, negotiated for him an appropriate (that is, noble and rich) marriage. It was then that Augustine left his concubine, but because the chosen girl was too young and a marriage would be delayed for a long time, he took a new concubine. He was inwardly unhappy, for as much as he attempted to become free from the questions and needs that tortured him, whenever he seemed to have reached the goal, he lost sight of it again.

Not without reason, however, his mother saw the fulfillment of her fond hope, the conversion and baptism of her son, coming closer and closer during these years. Augustine's intellectual development at this time was moving more and more in the direction of a much closer relationship to the church. He believed in the existence of God, to whom he clung through faith, in Christ, the Scriptures, "on whose side stands the authority of the Catholic church," and the way of salvation to which they point. But Augustine's question about the origin of evil remained: "What torments did my travailing heart then endure! What sights, O my God!"

Step by step the complete turn to Christianity took place: "By inward stings thou didst disturb me so that I was impatient." Augustine had already detached himself from Manicheism. The writings of Plotinus, which he read in a Latin translation, helped to acquaint him with the thinking of Plato which had been poured into new forms (called Neoplatonism), and gave him the certain knowledge of God as a non-bodily being who is true being, exalted above everything material. He also learned that evil is not a substance, as Manicheism taught, but the lack of true being, the separation from God. The questions which had tortured him since joining the Manichees were solved. And from the letters of Paul, in which he now steeped himself, he learned that the way to fellowship with God could be given only by God himself, through his grace.

"I had considered all thy works and trembled"; with these words Augustine concluded the seventh book of his *Confessions*. But so far only a new insight had been gained, not a new inner existence. Augustine could easily have relinquished his office as a rhetorician; it had been a burden for a long time, keeping him away, with its external business and its humiliations, from the true life. In addition, there was illness, which made the execution of his office difficult. But still he was imprisoned by his worldly mind, the striving for honor and success, and by the flesh.

The spiritual father of Ambrose, Simplicianus, set before his eyes the example of the rhetorician Marius Victorinus, through whose translations Augustine had come to know Neoplatonism. Simplicianus, who had met Victorinus in Rome and had subsequently become more familiar with him, was able to relate to Augustine from his own experience how Marius Victorinus had found the way to Christianity by the study of the Scriptures and had confessed it openly without regard to his office and his reputation among the pagans. In the persecutions of Emperor Julian he had even renounced his office rather than deny his faith. Augustine, on hearing this, was inflamed with the desire to imitate this example. But he was still too entangled in the world; two wills conflicted within him and tore his very soul apart.

Another conversation played a decisive role with him. A fellow African, Ponticianus, visited him. During the conversation he accidentally opened a book which was lying on the table close by and discovered to his joyful surprise that it contained the letters of Paul. Thus the conversation turned to questions of faith. Ponticianus, a zealous Christian, began to speak of Anthony the hermit, of whom Augustine had not yet heard. The report on the life of Anthony and the miracles which God worked through him deeply impressed Augustine and his friend Alypius. Ponticianus did not stop with this tale of the past, but went on to tell about the monasteries of the present and of that which he himself had experienced. At one time he had been in Treves, accompanying the emperor as an imperial official. On a free afternoon he had taken a walk in the gardens adjoining the city walls. Two of his friends, separated from him, had come upon a settlement of monks and had found there a copy of the biography of Anthony and immediately began to read it. At first filled with admiration, then with love, and at last with a definite decision, they immediately resigned their offices and joined the settlement of monks, leaving Ponticianus behind with a wondering heart.

This report deeply moved Augustine. He had before him an example of others who had taken the very step from which he had shrunk again and again. Beside himself, he called to his friend after Ponticianus had left: "What is this? What did you hear? The uninstructed start up and take heaven, and we—with all our learning but so little heart—just see where we wallow in flesh and blood! Because others have gone before us, are we ashamed to follow, and not rather ashamed at our not following?" Augustine rushed into the garden, carried away by inner excitement. He threw himself down under a fig tree and gave vent to his tears: "How long, how long? Tomorrow and tomorrow? Why not now? Why not this very hour make an end to my uncleanness?" A child's voice, singing and calling in the neighbor's house: "Pick it up, read it," seemed to give Augustine the answer. He took up the letters of Paul and read the first chapter he found on opening the book. It was Romans 13, where he read: "Let us conduct ourselves becomingly as in the day, not in reveling and drunkenness, not in debauchery and licentiousness, not in quarreling and jealousy. But put on the Lord Jesus Christ, and make no provision for the flesh, to gratify its desires." Augustine did not want to read on, and it was not necessary: "For instantly, as the sentence ended, there was infused in my heart something like the light of full certainty and all the gloom of doubt vanished away."

That was the conversion of Augustine. The wavering had ceased; worldly temptation was over. He reported to his friend Alypius, who confirmed him in his decision. Together they went to his mother Monica and told her what had happened. "She leaped for joy triumphant; and she blessed thee, O God." This took place in the fall of 386. With his mother, his son Adeodatus, Alypius, and a few other friends, Augustine retired into the quiet of the country estate Cassiciacum near Milan after a brief stay in the city to complete his teaching duties. On Easter of the next year, 387, he was baptized by Ambrose. On the journey back to Africa, Augustine's mother died in the Italian port of Ostia. But she could close her eyes peacefully because her son, who had caused her so much sadness, had found the focal point for his life.

His life moved in a straight direction from then on. At Cassiciacum he had begun to expound in philosophical writings what he had discovered. He continued to do so at Thagaste and began to win a reputation. When during a temporary stay in Hippo Regius in 391 the congregation there demanded him for its pastor, he hesitantly accepted the call. Serious study of the Scriptures prepared him for his profession, which for him meant the beginning of a new epoch. For now that which he knew on the basis of philosophical presuppositions had to be anchored ever more firmly in the Scriptures. The duties of the office drew Augustine increasingly deeper into an occupation with purely ecclesiastical questions and tasks. As the bishop of his diocese he soon became the unofficial ecclesiastical leader of Africa, and his influence extended far beyond the borders of his country.

Three main epochs characterized his life's work: the controversy with Manicheism, for which he was qualified as no one else; the fight against Donatism; and the controversy with Pelagius. A series of writings originated in connection with Pelagianism which cannot be discussed here. Nor can we discuss Augustine's numerous other writings, such as his *The City of God,* which has had an impact even beyond the church through the centuries. In a review of the year 427 Augustine counted ninety-three writings, not including his numerous sermons and letters. With Augustine a splendor engulfed the church of Africa as never before. But this splendor was, in a manner of speaking, an evening glow. When Augustine died on August 28, 430, the Vandals were already besieging his bishop's see. The Catholic church of Africa, which, since the days of Tertullian and Cyprian, had known how to preserve for itself a proud and independent position, equal to that of Rome, fell into an abyss right after Augustine's death. It never recovered from the blow inflicted on it by the rule of the Vandals.

PELAGIUS

The Adopted Heretic

Pelagius is known to the church of both the West and the East as a heretic and the father of heretics. Augustine is counted as one of the four great teachers (beside Ambrose, Jerome and Gregory the Great) of the Catholic church who rank just after the apostles and evangelists. And yet, when Pelagius appeared he could base his views on the practically unanimous statements of the whole church from its beginning to his own time. Augustine could at best base his on those of Tertullian and on some scattered remarks of Cyprian and Ambrose. Although the Catholic church praised Augustine highly and condemned Pelagius, it has absorbed much of Pelagius' thinking and basic attitudes, despite the fact that the controversy between Pelagius and Augustine went to the very heart of Augustine's theology, the doctrine of sin and grace.

What is Augustine's doctrine of sin and grace? God created man good. Man could not have remained sinless on his own, if God had not given man the grace which enabled him to achieve the fullness of blessedness. But the first man, with the free will given to him by God, turned from the good, followed the instigation of the serpent, and fell into sin. And with him we all have fallen, for we all were incorporated in that first man. That fall is known as original sin, and its burden is borne by newborn children even before they have committed their own sins. To this original sin is added actual sin, for since Adam's fall we are incapable of the good, and sinfulness has become our true substance. We cannot do other than sin.

Of what does sin consist? Here there are two lines of thought in Augustine. In the one line, the lower one, so to speak, sin is understood as fleshly, as lust in the true sense. But there is also another understanding in Augustine (which also is Luther's understanding): the essence of sin is the turning away from God, the exaltation of man above God, and the turning to man himself, the love of self, from which everything else follows. For the sake of this sin mankind is justly rejected by God, for this sin is much greater than we can imagine.

We would be condemned to death if God had not come to our assistance through his grace. Man cannot obtain grace by himself, for it would not be grace unless it were an unmerited gift. It is God who gives this grace, and he gives it to those whom he chooses according to his pleasure. The number of people destined for salvation is definitely fixed from the beginning. God knew from the beginning to whom he would give this grace. It is grace alone that counts; man can do nothing to earn it. The infusion of this grace is at the beginning of all things, and him to whom God gives it he also leads to salvation.

Because grace comes from God, it is also irresistible. It infuses in man the power which he needs to do good and to persevere in it, the love with which man can adhere to God in faith. By this grace man who is, so to speak, inwardly destroyed by sin is restored, and the image of God in him is renewed. He who stands in grace does good and perseveres in it until his blessed end. Only this perseverance to the end shows whether a man is truly called by God. Many fall away before that and prove by their falling that they just have not received from God the gift of perseverance. This grace of God comes to men not according to their merits but solely according to the unsearchable plan of God who calls some and condemns others, on the basis of his foreknowledge, not of what we will do but of what he will do.

Originally Augustine had believed, following the teaching of his predecessors, that the free will in man after the Fall still had the power to accept or to reject the grace of God. But soon he began to formulate the matter more sharply, as seen above: mankind is a sinful mass out of which God calls some to salvation; man is unable to do anything to influence God's choice. God is all and in all: if God does not have mercy on man, man wills and believes in vain. Only he to whom God turns in his unfathomable mercy can be saved. All others are condemned, destined by a knowing and willing God to destruction even before they have seen the light of the world, even before Adam fell.

Pelagius' views were opposed to these teachings of Augustine, and were endorsed by Caelestius, a Roman lawyer of noble ancestry. A third figure, Julian, the bishop of Eclanum, raised his voice as the leader of an opposition group. But they were not successful in their promotion of Pelagius' views and they were expelled from the church, even though a pope (Zosimus) and some synods (for example, a Palestinian synod in 415) endorsed their views. Augustine skillfully marshalled the authority and strength of his African synods, won Innocent I over to his side, and then persuaded Emperor Honorius to intervene against Pelagius and his like-minded supporters. When they went to the East, i.e., to Nestorius, their fate was sealed.

Cyril had Pelagianism condemned in Ephesus in 431 as a kind of favor to the West; in reality the East was on Pelagius' side and held to his teaching of the freedom of human will. Perhaps it never would have come to all these controversies if Pelagius and Caelestius had not left Rome (evidently because Alaric had conquered the city), and gone to Africa, where in 411 Caelestius wanted to be received into the clergy of Carthage. Up to that point Augustine had judged Pelagius rather kindly. He intentionally did not mention Pelagius' name in his writings on the doctrine of sin even when dealing with the matter. No doubt Pelagius had a good reputation, not only because of his scholarship, but especially because of his upright moral conduct. Incidentally, the dates of his birth and his death are unknown. It is believed that he came from Ireland.

The starting point of Pelàgius as well as of Caelestius was that Augustine's doctrine of sin and grace destroys the basis for the moral life—yet morality is the essence of Christianity. "Without hope for a reward for good works no one will be able to do good works." "We are unable to walk on the way of virtue unless hope accompanies us." Christ is given to us as a teacher and as an example, but what good does he do us if we are, as Augustine asserts, incapable of good on our own? The nature of man is good: that is the basic conviction of both Pelagius and Caelestius. If we see man do evil as well as good, this is no proof against his nature. One cannot speak of the existence of original sin; man is not forced to sin. Rather, at his birth he is capable of both good and evil. The dignity and honor of being a man consists precisely in the freedom to choose either side. Man is corrupted only by the long habit of sinning, and so it seems as if sin belongs to his nature.

Julian of Eclanum has summarized especially well the thinking of Pelagius, although he adds nothing really new: God, who has created the world and man, is good and just. Is it possible, then, that his creation has fallen into corruption? How can God reject a newborn child, who has had no opportunity for sin at all? The will is necessary for sinning. How can a newborn child have a will for sinning? If God is just, he can punish man only for something which he could have avoided. But if, according to Augustine, sin belongs to the nature of man and is unavoidable, how can God impute sin to him?

In Pelagius the traditional ecclesiastical piety rebelled against Augustine. It had demanded of the Christian the proof of moral deeds from the very beginning of the church. Characteristically, Pelagius had come from monasticism; and it was in monastic circles that even after Pelagius' death the opposition to Augustine's doctrine of grace continued. And indeed here the limit of Augustine's influence on the Catholic church is given, the unrestricted acceptance of the Augustinian doctrine of sin and grace that would have meant self-surrender for the church. It is true that Augustine's doctrine of original sin was accepted; the Pelagian resistance to this doctrine had no chance of triumph because infant baptism was a deeply entrenched custom of the church, and what purpose would baptism serve if not that of forgiveness of sins?

Augustine's assertion of the impossibility of sinless perfection of man in this life also won out because it definitely agreed with church doctrine. However, his assertion of the complete incapacity of man for the good was not accepted, not even during his lifetime. The doctrines of the grace of God which precedes human willing and doing and which works irresistibly; of God's predestination of the elect to salvation without their own achievements preceding it, and especially the view of God's predestination of others to destruction also were not accepted. It is characteristic that Jerome, although he passionately aligned himself with Augustine in the controversies over the doctrine of grace, did not understand the decisive parts of it at all and spoke naively of the free will which would rely in its good deeds upon the help of God. "God's grace *also* is important when he aids our will," he declared. Though he wrote this in opposition to Pelagius, the thought is closer to Pelagius than it is to Augustine.

Jerome's attitude is characteristic of the basic mood of the church of that time and of the Catholic church in general. The monks of southern Gaul rose up against Augustine, and the advocates of the Catholic concept of tradition, such as Vincent of Lerins, turned against the "new doctrines" of Augustine. They did not deny the necessity of God's grace, but that grace, they held, exists *in addition* to the human will. Even the energetic advocates of Augustinianism in that time did not dare or did not understand enough to advocate the full Augustinian doctrine of grace. Even Caesarius of Arles was in danger because of his defense of Augustine, although the synod of 529 under his leadership adopted a position between Augustine and Pelagius.

The conclusion to which Gregory the Great brought the controversies was acceptable not only because of the reputation which Gregory subsequently enjoyed, but also because it agreed with the inner nature of Catholicism. What he taught certainly sounded Augustinian, but ultimately it was removed from Augustine: some are elected by God, others are rejected. We cannot fathom why this is so; we have to leave it up to God; what he does is just. The good that we do belongs to God and us, "thus one may say that we deliver ourselves when we agree with God, who delivers us." This amounts to grace and man's deeds, God and man, not God alone. This has remained the basic attitude of Catholicism.

Although Augustine is frequently cited by Catholicism even today, it is always in an abbreviated fashion. As often as Catholicism speaks of the effect of grace, always the little word "and" is added, and if that addition usually is done secretly, then this is the effect of the Reformation and of Luther's doctrine of justification. Since the time of Gregory, when the Catholic church speaks of grace, it is referring to the grace that is mediated through the ecclesiastical institution of salvation. This is not the same as Augustine's conception and indicates how far the Catholic church's teaching on grace differs from that of the man who has been given the title "teacher of grace" by that church.

JOHN CHRYSOSTOM

The Goldenmouthed Preacher

Chrysostom is a Greek word which means "Goldenmouth." It was the name given John, the bishop of Constantinople, more than a thousand years ago. He received this name because of his sermons, hundreds of which have been preserved and handed down to us. Chrysostom was a voluminous writer (the thirteen large volumes of his writings that have come down to us make up the largest corpus of any of the theologians of the Greek church), as well as the most powerful preacher of the ancient church. He wove words together like no one before him and only few since. He made full use of his rhetorical training, and yet his effectiveness did not rest on that, but instead on his being rooted in the Scriptures. He brought the Bible to life and into life, whether he interpreted the biblical books continuously or preached on individual themes. He did not bend the Scriptures to suit his thoughts and desires; he did not impose his own thinking upon them, as did many of his time, and quite a few do today, but really interpreted them. And what he preached he also lived. Chrysostom (his surname has gained such weight that it has almost completely replaced his proper name and is used as such) was a shining light in the darkness of the Eastern church in the last quarter of the fourth century.

John Chrysostom was born around 350 at Antioch. His father, a high-ranking officer, died soon after his birth, and thus the youth of John was spent under the influence of his mother, who provided her son with an excellent education. But unlike Augustine's, the development of John followed a straight line. It appears that before he entered his chosen profession, law, he broke with the world so thoroughly that he no longer desired to keep even his church office as a lector. He withdrew into monasticism and spent six years in the loneliness of the mountains, at first as the disciple of an old monk who practiced extreme asceticism, then completely alone.

He went so far with his ascetic practices that he had to return to Antioch for medical help to restore his health. Now he could no longer withdraw from the call of his home church, and around 380 he was consecrated deacon and in 386 presbyter (pastor). For twelve years he held the pastorate at Antioch, years in which he became famous. From Antioch he was called to the most important but also most difficult office of the church of the East, that of the bishop of the capital of the empire, Constantinople. "Called" is not really the right word: he was forced into it. One day Chrysostom was invited to a meeting with the highest government official in a house outside of Antioch. Upon his arrival he was asked without further ado to take a seat in a waiting carriage, and soon he found himself in Constantinople, where he was consecrated bishop.

Some have attempted to explain this abduction by saying that the congregation at Antioch would not have released its preacher voluntarily. Chrysostom had acquired an extraordinary popularity in that city. What a preacher he was! There was a rebellion in Antioch in 387, caused by exorbitant taxation. There were riots in the streets, demonstrations, and destruction until the raging crowd finally toppled the statues of the imperial family and dragged them through the streets. The military had to use weapons to restore order. The courts started their work, and what was worse, reports about the events were dispatched by special couriers to Emperor Theodosius. How he reacted to such revolts is shown in his attitude a few years later to the rebellion in Thessalonica. A paralyzing terror fell on the Antiochians who had so recently been conscious of their strength. The streets were as if swept clean. Whoever was able left the city now threatened by the ire of the emperor; others hid themselves in their houses. It was Chrysostom who cared for the disheartened when everything else failed them. Of course the pagan philosophers had fled.

The famous orator Libanius wrote five speeches which deal with the events at Antioch. One of them is believed to have been delivered before the emperor to move him to immediate leniency. But this was only sham. Libanius took care not to go out on a limb, for the wrath of the emperor would likely strike those who dared to intercede for the evildoers. All these speeches were composed after everything was over. But it was quite different with Chrysostom; he stayed in the threatened city. This is more or less taken for granted of the pastor of a congregation and would not deserve special mention. But he also extended his pastoral care to all who despaired. He preached day after day, directly addressing himself to the subject of the day. Those were his famous "pillar sermons," which were given this name because of the overturned image pillars.

He did more than just speak comfortingly to the congregation, using standard clichés of optimism as it is sometimes customary to do in such circumstances. Chrysostom gave real comfort. He raised up the despondent and called them to behavior worthy of Christians. What had stricken the city, he said, was a deserved affliction for the sin of its inhabitants. He felt that this was the only way in which a Christian could grasp what had happened, and if he understood it as an exhortation to introspection, repentance, and a truly new way of life, it would be to his blessing. Away from the affliction of the day and to the Scriptures! That was the motto of Chrysostom.

It is understandable that a preacher who shared the affliction of his congregation and knew how to take care of his people would be highly esteemed by his congregation. At the same time Flavian, the bishop of Antioch, had hurried to court despite the winter season in order to appease the emperor. And indeed Antioch, in contrast to Thessalonica later, got away scot-free.

But the high esteem of his congregation could not have been the reason for the almost violent abduction of Chrysostom to Constantinople. Nor can the reason lie in the assumption that Chrysostom would have shied away from the responsibility and the burden of the bishop's office and would have to be forced to accept it. Indeed, there is probably some truth in that, just as certainly as the thought of the displeasure of the Antiochians would play a role when Chrysostom was spirited away so suddenly and secretly into the palace of the bishop of Constantinople. In all probability, however, church politics played the primary role.

In Constantinople Patriarch Nectarius had died, and many aspired to the vacant, extremely influential, and lucrative position. The bishop of Alexandria, Theophilus, in particular, sought the position, not for himself, but for one of his minions. If one of his partisans could become bishop of Constantinople, then he could become the supreme ruler of the whole church of the East. This ecclesio-political, and at the same time purely political, striving for power by the Alexandrian evidently met with the disapproval of the emperor's minister Eutropius, who at the time was all-powerful at the imperial court. He acted quickly and thoroughly, without wasting time with negotiations, let alone elections. When the Alexandrian bishop did not seem willing to accept the accomplished fact, Eutropius pointed with the necessary directness to the material about him which was filed at court and which would be more than sufficient to bring him to trial. With this Theophilus reluctantly gave in.

The occasion quickly presented itself by which Theophilus sought to overthrow Chrysostom, who was a hindrance to his plans. Chrysostom had been consecrated bishop of Constantinople in February of 398. In the year 403 he was removed from office and banished for the first time, but only for a short period. And a few months later the first banishment was followed by the second, and this time definite, removal and banishment. Chrysostom died on September 14, 407, as a result of afflictions intentionally imposed on him.

How did this happen? Chrysostom was a victim of the political intrigues going on in the Greek church which at the time were closely involved with state politics, since the church of the East was on its way to becoming the Byzantine state church. He had begun by executing his office with energy and intrepidity; such an approach was necessary but it also made things quite uncomfortable for many. Very little remained of the old simplicity which had prevailed among the clergy. In the bishop's palace pomp was at home: Chrysostom did away with the pomp. The clergy had grown accustomed to a comfortable life: Chrysostom sharply reminded them of the duties of their office. There were among them clergymen who lived like parasites in the palaces of the rich; they provided a coat of piety for their benefactors and an easy life for themselves. Unruly and undisciplined monks roamed about. There were bishops who had attained their office through bribery, and clergymen whose reputations were shady to say the least. All this ceased when Chrysostom became bishop. The monks had to return to their monasteries; all those who did not conform to the standards required by their spiritual office were unfrocked. At a synod in Ephesus Chrysostom deposed six bishops at one time because they had purchased their offices.

Thus Chrysostom won many bitter enemies for himself. That he himself lived according to the strictest standards did not impress them, and that he took care of the poor and built hospitals from the money that was saved, impressed them even less. They all were just waiting for an occasion to drive their disciplinarian from his position and to restore the old order of things. Chrysostom played right into their hands, for he was no politician and was interested only in whether something was right or wrong. He sharply reprimanded rich widows who, despite all their show of piety and their reputation as pillars of the church, lived more as worldlings than as Christians. Again and again he preached against wealth and luxury. He did not even shy away from attacks on the court when he considered it necessary. For this he soon fell from the favor of his former sponsor Eutropius. Ironically, however, Eutropius himself soon after fell from power, and only the intervention of Chrysostom protected him when he had to take sanctuary in the church from a raging mob which wanted to take revenge on their former tormentor. Chrysostom even went so far as to criticize the entourage of the empress. And with that he offered his opponents the opportunity to play the mighty Empress Eudoxia off against him.

Now Theophilus himself appeared on the field. Had not Chrysostom given quarters in Constantinople to Egyptian monks whom Theophilus had expelled from Egypt because they would not disavow Origen? Did not this make Chrysostom a protector of dogmatic errors? Although the attempt to prove this was not successful, Theophilus gathered into a "synod" all the ecclesiastical opponents of Chrysostom who could be found and charged that Chrysostom had, contrary to ecclesiastical regulations, interfered in the affairs of other dioceses. That was the point of the charge which could, to a certain extent, be clothed with the appearance of legality; everything else was completely without foundation.

But no one was supposed to ask what the Alexandrian and his followers, who came mostly from other dioceses, had to do in the affairs of the church in Constantinople. Chrysostom refused to appear before this synod. Because of this refusal and his contempt of the synod, that body deposed him. The emperor, who was persuaded that Chrysostom had insulted the empress, confirmed this verdict. Thus Chrysostom was forced into exile.

But he had hardly left Constantinople when he was recalled. The superstitious empress had been frightened by an accident which she took to be a punishment from God for the unjust banishment of Chrysostom. However, this fright did not last long. As her fright waned, the insinuations of Chrysostom's opponents had more success. When the bishop complained in a sermon about the noise of a celebration close to the church which was disturbing the service, sentence was definitely passed on him. The festival about which he complained was being held to celebrate the erection of a silver statue dedicated to the empress. This renewed "lese majesty" was the occasion for the final removal of the bishop from office, although the reason given was that after his removal by the synod under Theophilus, he had resumed his office in an irregular way.

The followers of Chrysostom were not ready to concede to the injustice that had been done to their bishop, and it was necessary to proceed against them with force. Services were disturbed, and other similar incidents took place. Chrysostom, despite his banishment to Armenia, kept up the relationship with his congregation and his friends by letters. Now the West began to protest against his unjustified removal from office. The controversies which ensued would fill an unpleasant chapter by themselves and finally led to a rupture of church fellowship between Rome and Constantinople. For these reasons the deportation of the bishop to the remotest part of the empire, the Caucasus, was arranged. He had to travel on foot, and after three months his enemies accomplished their goal: Chrysostom succumbed to the strain of the march.

Thirty years later his body was returned to Constantinople and buried on January 27, 438, with solemn pomp and the participation of the entire imperial court in the Church of the Apostles. But this posthumous restoration could not undo the injustice which Constantinople had inflicted on its greatest bishop, especially because subsequently the way of Theophilus and not that of Chrysostom was chosen.

NESTORIUS

A New Controversy

The overthrow of Chrysostom was, as we saw, caused by the struggles for power in the Eastern church during the last part of the fourth century. Under Theophilus, Alexandria successfully eliminated Constantinople as a competitor and sustained its own hegemony. This effort was continued by the successors of Theophilus, Cyril and Dioscurus. Thus the ecclesiastical controversies of the fifth century, with which we usually associate these men, may well be seen under the heading of these power struggles; and the controversy about the doctrine of the two natures of Christ, which was supposedly the crucial issue, may be considered of secondary importance at most.

But this would be an oversimplification of the situation. Actually, the Christological controversies, as they are called, debated a question which went beyond pure theology into the depths of faith. These controversies were inevitable and came over the church of the East with inherent necessity, for they grew out of the Arian controversies. What makes these controversies so distasteful to us is the fact that the human element could not be separated from the questions which were so important to theology and the life of faith. The churches of the East which participated in these controversies had to pay dearly: in Egypt and the adjacent areas the churches were destroyed by internal dissension and overcome by a creeping inner paralysis.

The controversies lasted approximately 300 years. They began with Apollinaris of Laodicea who was installed as bishop of Laodicea about 361. Apollinaris had written on Christological questions since 352, and he raised new questions even before the Arian controversy had fully ended. It is true that his views were condemned several times by synods but, on the whole, his views were discussed only marginally during his lifetime. Even the three Cappadocians had no basic understanding of them, let alone a solution to them. The times just were not ripe for it; first of all the Arian controversy had to be settled.

In the Arian controversy, the main concern originally was to determine how the coexistence and relationship of the persons of the Trinity should be described. The question centered on the divinity of Christ, on the assertion that Christ is of the same essence as God. But as soon as this was determined and the question of the Trinity was decided, another question necessarily followed: how is the humanity of Christ to be combined with his divinity? So we see the Christological controversies develop as soon as the Arian controversy was brought to a solution in 381 at Constantinople. The full divinity of Christ had to be secured in order to guarantee the salvation of mankind. For only if Christ was really God in the full meaning of the word could his work effect man's salvation. But by the same token it was just as necessary for Christ to be a true man! For how can a purely divine being save us, who are so completely human? Yet, how could the full humanity be conceived as united with the full divinity in the one Jesus Christ? How could both be combined harmoniously with each other?

These were the issues at stake. There were two opposing parties. On the one side there was the scientific theology, represented by the theologians of the so-called Antiochian school: Diodorus of Tarsus, Theodore of Mopsuestia, Theodoret of Cyrus, Ibas of Edessa, and several others (Chrysostom was one). They were the "left wing" in these controversies. But they were defeated, or they appeared to be defeated, for almost all were, at least for a time, stamped as heretics by the church, and some are known as heretics to this day. This is especially true of Nestorius, whose fall marked the fall of the whole school.

The theologians of the Antiochian school all thought historically. They attempted to comprehend the literal meaning of the Scriptures by interpreting them historically and renouncing the allegorical interpretation of those theologians influenced by Origen. Their starting point was the man Jesus of whom the Gospels tell. This Jesus is equal to God (*homoousios*); he is Christ, but not in such a way that by being Christ his humanity is swallowed up in his divinity. The man remains; God takes up residence in him. The separateness of the two natures in Christ, the divine and the human, was carefully maintained. Their view was clear and perceptive. The danger inherent in it was that the two natures would make themselves independent and that this would result in a double person of Christ. For although they could speak clearly of the two natures, it was difficult for them to portray and to imagine how these two natures could form a unity in the one person of Christ.

On the right wing were the Egyptian theologians for the most part. One cannot say unequivocally that they were continuing the lines of Athanasius. He was much too much occupied with the fight to establish the divinity of Christ within the Trinity and too little a theologian in the full sense of the word to think through completely the question of the relationship of the two natures in Christ. But one will have to say that the Egyptian theologians, especially Cyril of Alexandria, fought for the same beliefs which Athanasius had advocated in his day. They all had a conception of the salvation of man completely different from that of the Antiochians. According to the Antiochians man is saved by the exertion of the moral will and his human nature is exalted, whereas with Athanasius and the Egyptian theologians involved in the Christological controversy, man and his nature are drawn into the deity; man is made divine, so to speak. Thus for them everything depends on the divinity of Jesus Christ, on his divine nature.

This concern was expressed in different ways. Where it was done radically, as with Apollinaris of Laodicea and later with the so-called Monophysites (the word comes from the Greek and means advocates of the doctrine of one nature), only the one nature, the divine, remained, while the human was relegated completely to the background. Where it was not conceived and described so sharply and drastically, as for instance by Cyril of Alexandria, one could still speak of the two natures. Here we see the difference between the Egyptians and the Antiochians. The latter were clearly aware of the two natures and had only a pale or quite theoretical picture of their unity. The Egyptians, on the other hand, emphasized the unity so explicitly that practically only the one, the divine nature, existed. The human nature became an empty form which they talked about but did not know what to do with theologically.

The shortcomings are clear on both sides: with the Antiochians the divinity of Christ was in danger of being forgotten, with the Egyptians, his humanity. Yet there had to be a solution which would give both natures their due. For Jesus Christ was God and man at the same time, not mere man who was exalted to God or God in an apparent body. Neither party wanted to advocate either view, for both had been proven errors. But neither side was ready to abandon its presupposition, for to do so would have led necessarily to certain dangerous consequences. It was just as in the Arian controversy where the question was how the divinity of Christ can be brought into harmony with the doctrine of the one God. Two different conceptions vied with each other; each embodied a basically different concept of Christianity. Now the issue was how the fact that Christ was God in the full meaning of the word can be combined with the fact that he was at the same time fully man. And again we see two basically opposite conceptions of Christianity at loggerheads with each other.

This is what was behind the controversies which for three centuries disturbed the church of the East. The West was more involved this time than it had been in the Arian controversy. These controversies were not concluded until a solution was found down to the last detail, that is, as far as a full answer is at all possible in such questions. This is evidence that the Christological controversy was a real debate about theological questions and not just a power struggle carried out under the guise of doctrine.

The real controversy began with a conflict between Bishop Cyril of Alexandria and Bishop Nestorius of Constantinople. Cyril was successor and nephew to Theophilus. In the year 412 he ascended the bishop's throne, evidently with the definite intention of subjecting Constantinople to the authority of Alexandria as his uncle had successfully begun to do. Theophilus had brought Chrysostom, who belonged to the Antiochian school, to ruin. Why could Cyril not succeed in doing the same with Nestorius, also an Antiochian, who had ascended the bishop's throne of Constantinople in 428? And indeed Cyril achieved his goal even faster than had Theophilus. It had taken the latter five years to remove Chrysostom; Cyril accomplished it in three with Nestorius. We do not have to explain with whom our sympathies lie. They lie with Nestorius. For Cyril, just as Theophilus before him, worked by dishonest means, and Nestorius, just as Chrysostom before him, manifested an attitude which cannot but impress us.

When Nestorius came to Constantinople he found the city embroiled in a controversy over the veneration of Mary. The reputation of Mary had been increasing constantly in the course of the first centuries. The New Testament had still spoken naively of Mary's other children and of the fact that she at first did not believe in Jesus. (This is the only way to interpret the passages concerned, all other interpretations are contrived. The Catholic claim that the brothers of Jesus were children of Joseph by a former marriage, not only lacks support in the New Testament, it also is opposed by the ancient church itself. Tertullian, for instance, spoke unabashedly of the brothers and sisters of Jesus as children of Mary.)

Slowly but surely the reputation of Mary grew and the qualities attributed to her increased until at the time of Nestorius she had been exalted by many to the position of the virginal mother of

God. The controversy in Constantinople centered around the question: how should one speak of Mary? Was she the "Bearer of God" or the "Bearer of a man"? Linguistically the words are not pleasing to the ear, but the corresponding Greek words have to be translated in this way. One could also say "Mother of God" and "Mother of a man," but this is not exact enough. It is doubtful whether all those who took part in the argument knew what the theological issue was.

For the theologians, in any case, the matter was clear. Mary, of course, had given birth to a man, the Antiochians asserted, for the mere thought that a man could bring God himself into the world is absurd and ridiculous. But it was different with those who adhered to the thinking prevalent in Alexandria. The Alexandrians spoke of the "Bearer of God." Through Mary, the Logos, that is, God, was born as far as his humanity is concerned.

Nestorius at first rushed zealously into the controversy and spoke out against the term "Bearer of God" as a heretical error. Behind this term he sensed adherence to the beliefs of Apollinaris which the church had condemned long before. But when he had to concede that this was not at all the case, he relinquished his position and acknowledged the relative justification of this way of speaking. For one could not say that Mary had borne a mere man, but rather God was in him. To that extent one might also speak of Mary as the "Bearer of God" if one understood it correctly. But it would be better not to use the two controversial terms at all, and to use in their place a third one: "Bearer of Christ." This third term described the facts correctly and expressed the mystery of Christ rightly.

Except for Cyril, the controversy might have ended. He saw his opportunity. Although he spared neither effort nor expense to present himself in a favorable light at the imperial court, where he always had a representative, he found himself in the position of the accused. And his opponents, on whose side the emperor seemed to be, had suggested Nestorius as the judge! This was not surprising, for often we find the bishop of Constantinople playing this role because of his closeness to the imperial court. But Cyril must have been extremely bitter at the thought that his competitor should be the one to pass judgment on him.

In this moment Cyril used the weapon which his predecessor Theophilus had used against Chrysostom, but in vain. He accused Nestorius of being a heretic. It was natural for Cyril to oppose Nestorius and to be on the side of those who spoke of the "Bearer of God" exactly in the sense in which Nestorius rejected the term. If he could succeed now in stamping Nestorius a heretic for the views he advocated in his sermons he had sent to Cyril, he could with one stroke overcome the danger which threatened him at the moment and undermine Constantinople's reputation and that of the Antiochian theologians as well. Thus Cyril endeavored to win the imperial court, particularly the Roman bishop, over to his side.

At first he was not successful in Constantinople, but was very much so in Rome. For one thing Alexandria and Rome had long been allies. More important was the fact that Cyril knew how to deal with the Roman bishop. He approached him humbly as the arbiter in all important questions and requested his decision on whether he could still maintain fellowship with Nestorius. He then presented a description of the supposed teachings of Nestorius in which the latter would not have recognized himself. He also added some malicious slander to his presentation. Cyril knew that he was lying but the Roman bishop did not, and he reacted promptly. A synod gathered in 430 in Rome and instructed Cyril to demand of Nestorius a recantation of his error within ten days. If he refused, he should be excommunicated from the church. This was all declared without saying anything on the subject in question, of which the Romans understood little, or the supposed errors of Nestorius. The synod's decision was proclaimed to the whole world. Indeed, Nestorius, too, had written to Rome, but he wrote as an equal, and in such a way that it could seem that he was taking the side of the Pelagians who had fled from Rome to Constantinople. In so doing he could make only a negative impression on Rome.

Cyril used to good advantage the general authorization which had been given to him so lightly by Rome. At a synod in Alexandria he once more solemnly condemned Nestorius and demanded that Nestorius accept twelve theses formulated by Cyril. In effect, Cyril was practically demanding that Nestorius submit to the teachings of Cyril or else be excommunicated. But this was only a prelude. A General Council was called to convene in Ephesus at Pentecost, 431. Here the final decision would be made. Cyril prepared himself thoroughly for the council. He sought allies in advance. He found them in Bishop Memnon of Ephesus and in the bishop of Jesusalem. Memnon and the bishops of Asia Minor sensed a favorable opportunity to free themselves from the supremacy of Constantinople, and the bishop of Jerusalem had the same plans in regard to Antioch. It was clear to every expert in church politics that Antioch would come under attack along with Nestorius.

Since the local bishop was unfriendly toward Nestorius, his situation was difficult from the beginning. Naturally Memnon spread propaganda against Nestorius, so that at his arrival he found the populace incited against him and all the churches closed to him. The Antiochian theologians had noticed that danger was imminent, but evidently they had not realized its extent. They arrived belatedly in Ephesus where, in the meantime, Cyril had taken matters into his own hands. He had appeared, contrary to the imperial regulation, with a great entourage, as did Memnon. A large number of other bishops was already present, but the president of the council, John of Antioch, had not yet arrived. Then Cyril opened the synod on his own initiative. It did not disturb him that the imperial representative, whom the emperor had sent as his ambassador, and other bishops protested that he did not have any right to open the council. The council was simply in session; whoever did not appear—this included Nestorius and quite a few others—had to look after himself. "With frequent tears," as it says in the proclamation, they had already determined that "our Lord Jesus Christ, blasphemed by Nestorius," gave order "by this holy synod" that Nestorius, "the new Judas," should be removed and excluded from his spiritual office, when finally John of Antioch arrived in Ephesus and opened the true, rightful synod in the presence of the imperial commissar.

According to the regulations valid at the time, the synod presided over by John cannot be called anything but the true, rightful synod, although it had less participants than the one presided over by Cyril and Memnon. In John's synod things went as was to be expected: Cyril and Memnon were removed from office because they had opened the synod without authorization and their followers were excommunicated. The real doctrinal question was not debated at all. After all of this, the papal delegates from Rome also arrived. Of course, they participated in the synod of Cyril and joined in the condemnation of Nestorius.

Here we see what really happened at the Third Ecumenical Council which was to become so famous. Both groups had appealed to the emperor; his would be the final decision. The legal situation was clear. But Cyril knew how to support his cause. In Ephesus he had known how to influence the population by means of heralds and wall posters. Before the emperor there appeared now an abbot, accompanied by a tremendous and excited crowd, famous for his exemplary saintliness, who had made one of his rare excursions from the monastery in order to speak on behalf of Cyril and for the condemnation of Nestorius. What was the emperor's judgment? He declared both parties in the right, confirmed the sentences of removal imposed by both synods and arrested Nestorius as well as Cyril and Memnon.

Naturally nothing was decided by such a procedure, and therefore both groups reappealed to the emperor. But gradually the scales tipped in favor of Cyril. Nestorius, not sufficiently supported by the Antiochians, resigned and retired to a monastery. Cyril on the other hand gained freedom for himself, as did Memnon. Both had their bishoprics restored to them. The synod was officially closed, and the first act of the Christological controversy was over.

DIOSCURUS

The Person of Christ

The Council of Ephesus had ended in a complete victory for Cyril. This victory has to be attributed to the unscrupulous way in which Cyril pursued his goal. It is significant that Cyril's successor, Dioscurus, found the Alexandrian treasury empty because Cyril had paid so many bribes at the imperial court. But the nearsightedness of the Antiochian theologians was just as responsible for Cyril's triumph. They had abandoned Nestorius, consented to the controversial formula "Bearer of God," and signed a compromising theological formula, desired by the emperor, who wanted the controversies settled. They were able to sign the formula in good conscience, for it was so vague that even Nestorius would have been able to sign it.

However, the Antiochians should never have agreed to the condemnation of Nestorius. They sacrificed him for the sake of peace. But in condemning him they condemned themselves, for they thought and taught exactly as he did. Their weakness was soon to haunt them, for the hotheads on the other side were not satisified with the condemnation of Nestorius; in addition they demanded the condemnation of Diodorus of Tarsus and Theodore of Mopsuestia, both of whom had been the teachers of Nestorius. These men had taught not only Nestorius, but other Antiochian theologians as well.

At first it appeared that the Antiochians had acted rightly in abandoning Nestorius for tactical reasons. For although Nestorius was succeeded to the bishopric of Constantinople by some one of like mind with Cyril, on his death, another Antiochian theologian, Flavian, came to power in the capital of the empire. Elsewhere, too, Antiochians acquired new and important positions. Thus it seemed that the old influence had been regained. But appearances were deceiving. The attack of Dioscurus was soon to show how weak the position of the Antiochians really was. And when Dioscurus was finally rebuffed in the decision of the Council of Chalcedon, the strength of the Antiochians was exhausted and they were no longer in a position to take advantage of the possibilities which offered themselves.

Dioscurus was cut from the same cloth as his predecessor. As soon as he became bishop of Alexandria on the death of Cyril in 444, he took pains to repress even more the influence of the Antiochian theologians. He used every means of intrigue at his disposal. But he did not succeed, for all he could do was to look on as the Antiochians gained ground in Constantinople and elsewhere. When the new bishop of Constantinople dared to remove one of the adherents of the Egyptian party, Dioscurus regarded it as a declaration of war. He dropped all subterfuge and waged all-out war against the Antiochians.

This raised the curtain on the second act of the Christological controversies. Let us review once more their course so far. They began with the controversies which raged around Apollinaris of Laodicea. In trying to defend the position of Athanasius, Apollinaris had overdrawn the statements about Christ to such an extent that Christ's divinity was safeguarded, but his humanity was greatly restricted. "It is impossible that Christ was man in the full measure," declared Apollinaris. "Two complete things cannot become one." If Christ is God—and there can be no doubt that he is that, for everything depends on his divinity, which alone can save mankind—then he cannot have been man in the full sense. Rather we have to imagine that God assumed flesh, that is, the

Logos clothed himself in a human frame within the womb of Mary. Therefore, in the body of Christ the Logos took the place of the soul or of reason, as Apollinaris later put it. In this way the intention of Athanasius was achieved and the salvation of man was guaranteed through his deification, that is, as soon as he became a participant of the God-Logos who had become flesh in Christ.

But on the other hand, the salvation which he wanted to safeguard so completely had become extremely questionable: for the divinity can save only that which it has assumed. (This was already noted by Gregory of Nazianzus.) Both man's body and his soul or reason have to be saved, for it is precisely reason and will which lead the body to sin. But if, as Apollinaris asserted, Christ does not have a human soul or reason, how can he save men? Thus, instead of securing man's salvation Apollinaris endangered it by his Monophysitic solution, which for all practical purposes attributed only a divine nature to Christ.

It soon became apparent that Apollinaris' solution was untenable. Even in Egypt those who like Cyril had a better theological education saw its weaknesses. Thus it was relatively easy to eliminate Apollinaris' ideas on the official level without a great struggle. However, under the surface his thought remained as powerful as before. We clearly see this in the age of Dioscurus and afterwards. This first epoch, which also is called the Apollinarian controversy, was just a prelude. The real struggles began in the time of Cyril and Nestorius, as we saw in the preceding chapter. These controversies were so vehement because they were a cover for power struggles within the church. In reality Cyril, like the Antiochians, sought to maintain the full humanity of Jesus. He did not limit his humanity, as Apollinaris had done, even though he also moved in that direction. According to Cyril, the Logos had become flesh, man in the full sense with all his qualities. But even if the two natures are not mixed with each other, or the one changed into the other, still a unified being results from them in which both natures are merged into an indissoluble unity. The Logos became flesh so that if one speaks of Christ, one always speaks of the whole Christ, and what is asserted of his human nature also refers to his divine nature. Cyril always saw the *unity;* a separate concept of the two natures was not possible for him, and everything was seen under the heading of the salvation of man, who, in the Lord's Supper, becomes a participant in the incarnate Logos Christ and by it is drawn into him.

It is clear that Cyril, even if only theoretically, accepted the two natures. But as soon as his presuppositions were forgotten or over-simplified the result was inevitably a return to a one-nature teaching, that is, to Monophysitism, with all its consequences. At the time of Dioscurus such a development took place when a partisan of his, Eutyches, crossed the narrow line that separated the views of Cyril from Monophysitism. Dioscurus immediately took up the defense of Eutyches who was the abbot of a large monastery near Constantinople, and closely connected with influential men at the imperial court. According to Eutyches Christ did consist of two natures, but only before the uniting of the two in the incarnation of the Logos: "for the period after that I confess only one nature." Furthermore, he declared that the flesh of Christ and that of man are not of one essence. This view not only went far beyond what could be expected of Antiochian theology, it actually denied what Cyril had always maintained and even explicitly defended. But that did not matter to Dioscurus. He either did not understand or did not want to understand that Eutyches had overstepped the borders of church doctrine; he saw only that Eutyches had been removed by Bishop Flavian of Constantinople.

That happened in 448 after a special synod had been convened for this purpose. Dioscurus evidently considered this as a challenge addressed to him and immediately prepared to answer it. He had been interested for a long time in humiliating the Antiochians who, in his opinion, had become much too bold. He turned to the emperor and succeeded in having a new ecumenical council convened. Ephesus was chosen again for the meeting place, and Dioscurus was appointed council president. At the same time the

members of the Synod of Constantinople of 448, which had removed Eutyches, were not permitted to vote at the synod, and the
spokesman of the Antiochians was completely excluded from its
sessions. This arrangement suggested what could be expected of
the synod. But Dioscurus was able to surpass even the worst ex-
pectations. With good reason this council came to be called the
"Robber Synod" by Pope Leo I, who felt himself most horribly
mistreated by it, and by later historians. The person and the teaching of Eutyches were the subject of the negotiations. More than
four fifths of the delegates declared him orthodox: "Condemned
is everyone who, after the incarnation, still speaks of two natures,"
was the motto of the synod which was characterized by noisy
tumults in which the Antiochian theologians could not obtain the
floor. Nor could the doctrinal letter of Leo I, which had been
delivered by three papal delegates, be read. Eutyches was restored
to his office, but his bishop, Flavian, as well as all the other leading Antiochian theologians, was removed and sent into exile. The
vacant bishops' sees were filled with followers of Dioscurus or of
adherents to Cyril's views. An Alexandrian clergyman, who until
now had acted as the ambassador of Dioscurus at the imperial
court, received the bishopric of Constantinople.

Not even Cyril had achieved such success. In 431 the battle had
gone both ways for a time until the victory finally fell to Cyril.
This time the victory of Dioscurus was assured from the beginning;
the opponent had been defeated completely without being able to
defend himself. And all that without the assistance of the Roman
pope, which Cyril had needed! They not only got along without
him, they even kept him within his appropriate limits. Dioscurus,
in effect, was now master of the church. With the help of Emperor
Theodosius II, who backed all his measures, Dioscurus was able
to carry through in the church of the East practically everything he
desired, and he made use of this power.

But that did not last long; Dioscurus had overplayed his hand.
As soon as a successor to the weak Theodosius II assumed the
throne it became apparent that Dioscurus' opponents had only been

temporarily defeated. In Syria, Asia Minor, and other areas, the Antiochian party had indeed lost its leaders (Flavian, for instance, had died in exile), but it continued to exist as a strong opposition group. The highly insulted Leo I, in particular, persisted in demanding a revision of the decisions of 449. He demanded that a council be held in Italy so that he might decide the controversial questions which he regarded as still open because he had had no opportunity to take a position. To an extent he was justified in looking at matters in this way since Flavian, along with others who had been removed in the year 449, had appealed to him.

Theodosius II died in 450 and was succeeded by his sister Pulcheria, who ruled with General Marcian. Immediately after her accession ecclesiastical politics began to take a completely new course. The restoration of peace with the West was a pressing matter, and besides, the bishop of Alexandria had become much too powerful. A council was convened, not in Italy as Leo had originally desired, but in Chalcedon, the sphere of immediate influence of the court. It was called together under a completely different set of circumstances. First, a synod excommunicated Eutyches and recalled the exiled Antiochian bishops. That was clear enough, and the bishops who appeared in large number to take part in the Council immediately knew which way the wind was blowing.

The council of Chalcedon, which was controlled by the imperial delegate, and which met from October 8 to November 4, 451, was not a very inspiring affair. In 449 at Ephesus and in the succeeding period, the bishops had stood on the side of the victorious Dioscurus; now they agreed with the same zeal with the opposite opinion of Leo I, which predominated in the council. From the beginning the removal of Dioscurus was a foregone conclusion. And no one defended him; instead, his former followers rapidly deserted him. The same noisy scenes took place as at the Robber Synod.

Seen from this point of view, the council, the fifteen-hundredth anniversary of which was celebrated a few years ago, offered no cause for commemoration. Dioscurus, who was accused of being a blasphemer of the Trinity, a heretic, a ravisher of relics, a thief, murderer, and other similar things, was removed and condemned for disobedience to the synod, for when he saw how the tide was running he no longer attended its sessions despite several summonses.

As high as Dioscurus had ascended in 449, so deep did he now fall. The striving of the Alexandrian bishops for power over the Eastern church, sought by every means for over three generations, had finally failed. In the following two centuries the events in the church of Egypt occupied the leaders of church and state. But more and more these events had only local significance until finally the Egyptian church, as well as several other churches of the East, began to lead an isolated existence alongside the Greek church.

Chalcedon was the starting point of that situation, for the council did not limit itself to a revision of the personality-oriented decisions of the Council of Ephesus in 449; rather, it made a doctrinal decision which was intended to put an end to the Christological controversies just as the Council of Constantinople in 381 had put an end to the Arian controversies. In size alone it was impressive: no less than six hundred bishops had been summoned, almost exclusively from the East. Once and for all the confession to be adopted by the synod, according to the repeated demand of the emperor, was supposed to clarify the controversial questions and bridge the opposing views. This was done as far as possible. The extremes were rejected and great effort was taken to reconcile West and East. That means that the attempt was made to reduce the theses which had been promulgated by the doctrinal letter of Leo I, which were rather close to those of the Antiochians, to one common denominator with those of Cyril.

It was declared that Jesus Christ is very God and very man. He is consubstantial with the Father, according to his divinity, consubstantial with us men, sin only excepted, according to his humanity. He is confessed to be in two natures, "unconfusedly, immutably, indivisibly, inseparably." In Christ both natures come together, uniting into one person, but not thereby eliminating their differences. The property of each nature was preserved. But this Christ in (not of) two natures is one, "one and the same Son and only-begotten, God the Word, our Lord Jesus Christ." That was the essential content of the formula of Chalcedon, which was solemnly proclaimed on October 25, 451 in the presence of the emperor.

Did it really solve the Christological controversy? Yes and no. We could say that it effected a solution in the same way that Constantinople had brought about the solution of the Arian controversies. On the one hand we see that from now on, at least for large areas of the East and of the West, it was unambiguously stated that he who speaks of Christ speaks of him as God and as man at the same time, in whom both are combined into an inseparable unity, and that neither can have precedence over the other. On the other hand we see that here only a formula, not a solution, is offered, a formula which declares that a kind of duality exists, but not how the duality is to be understood as unity. That is the result of the West's influence. Since Tertullian the West had been accustomed to think along the lines of this formula and stopped short, in contrast to the East, without feeling the desire to understand the content of the formula to its last detail. Likewise the solution of the Council of Constantinople of 381 remains just a formula when it speaks of one substance and three modes of existence of God in the Trinity.

But can it be different? The nature of God and the nature of Christ go beyond the limits of human knowledge. Here one has to stop and acknowledge the mystery; one has to concede that our knowledge is piecemeal and all our wisdom is stammering. Full understanding can come only after our perfection, and then it will no longer be understanding, but worship.

LEO 1

The Papacy—A Finished Product

The West had played a lively role in that aspect of the Christo-logical controversy which involved Dioscurus. At an earlier date, at the time of Cyril, it had been unable to do that. At that time Rome had also sent delegates to the Council of Ephesus (431), but Cyril had made all the important decisions before the papal delegates arrived, and they had little choice other than to give their belated assent. But they gave it in such a way as to imply that the synod had simply verified a previous decision of the pope. As far as the East was concerned the words of the papal delegates were empty. This attitude was shared by Cyril and other council participants, who used the Romans only to reinforce their own rather insecure position.

Cyril had "informed" Caelestinus I in a letter about Nestorius, and when Caelestinus responded by immediately condemning Nestorius in accordance with Cyril's wishes, the pope was really surrendering his freedom of action. Indeed, in his writing to Cyril he made it look as if the latter had seriously appealed to him and asked for his judgment, and as though the pope would render a decision only on the condition that Cyril execute it in the pope's stead and under his authority. But this did not worry Cyril. He had won the Roman see to his side, and that was his main concern. If beyond that he had received a blanket authorization against Nestorius, so much the better. He made unscrupulous use of it and deposed Nestorius although he was quite aware that only a council had the right to act in this way.

Thus at that time the Roman bishop, despite all the fine words, had let himself be taken in tow by the crafty Alexandrian and had helped to condemn a man whose theology was much more akin to that of the West than the theology of Cyril. This happened because he could not, or would not, discern clearly enough the points at issue and also because he did not have a talent for diplomatic maneuvering. All this had changed by the time of Dioscurus. Not Caelestinus I but Leo I sat on the throne of Peter in Rome.

Even before the synod of 448 removed him from office, Eutyches had attempted to win the pope over to his side and to report the controversy to him. When he was removed from office he increased his efforts. But Leo I refused to commit himself, saying that he would have to hear the arguments of the other side before reaching a decision. At first the reports from this other party were not completely satisfactory to Leo, as had once been the case with Nestorius. It was only when Flavian saw that he was in real danger that he adopted the tone of deference and humility which Leo wanted and which accorded with his understanding of the position of the Roman bishop. Leo quickly realized that he would have to side with Flavian and not with Dioscurus. But he did not make his decision without careful analysis as Caelestinus I had done. Moreover, he upheld what he considered to be the theologically correct position in spite of the fact that external circumstances made such a position very difficult.

The "Robber Synod" was a catastrophe for Flavian and the Antiochians, but it was also a crushing defeat for Leo I. He had prepared a grandiose theological document and had sent a delegation to the synod. (His doctrinal epistle, which played such a large role in Chalcedon, was originally written for the synod of 449.) But his delegates were almost ignored and were limited to a short introductory address on the agenda. When the vote against Flavian was being taken they were able to make a comment, but, ironically enough, because of linguistic and other misunderstandings, they seemed to be in agreement with the synod. Their most important contribution was the vocal interruption "We protest" at the proclamation of the condemnation of Flavian and his friends. The papal delegate only managed to get away by the skin of his teeth and had to return to Rome without his luggage. No wonder Leo worked with all strength to annul this synod. It was small comfort to him that Innocent I had fared much worse when he sent a delegation in favor of Chrysostom to Constantinople.

However, Leo's efforts to annul this synod met with great success. The fact that Flavian and the other Antiochians who had been deposed had asked for his intervention and appealed to him was quite a victory for the pope. Even more significant was the success at Chalcedon itself. Leo had sent a strong delegation to Chalcedon in order to forestall right at the outset the mishaps of Ephesus. The result was that his doctrinal epistle became the official confessional statement of the whole church. This had never before happened to a theological utterance of a Roman bishop. In addition, Leo's delegates were able to advance the pope's claim to a superior position and, when the imperial representatives were not present, they assumed the leadership of the council.

Nevertheless, many things did not go as Leo would have desired. That a council took place at all, and that it took place in the East and not on Italian soil as he had demanded originally, was not to his satisfaction. He thought that his doctrinal letter and his other promulgations had decided everything so that a council was superfluous. At the council itself not all the demands of his delegates were accepted. In particular, they were unable to prevent the last of the council's decisions, in which the same honors were ascribed to the bishop of Constantinople as to the bishop of Rome, although the former was to rank second. That was completely unacceptable to Leo I, but he had to accept it.

In the years after 541 even the validity of the confession of Chalcedon was seriously endangered by the ever widening influence of the Monophysites. Even the claim of Leo I to dominance over the East remained a theory; in reality he was unable to impose his will on the church of the East, which henceforth followed a course of development independent of the West.

Later ages have praised Chalcedon and the role played by Leo I. To medieval Latin Christendom, which had lost all control over the Eastern church, Leo's accomplishment at Chalcedon appeared to be a great feat. But if we want to evaluate Leo and understand his greatness we have to look to the West rather than to the East. Here we have standards by which to judge. Take the African church, of which we have spoken so often, for example. In the middle of the forties Leo sent an apostolic vicar to Africa with instructions to investigate the legality of some of the bishops' elections there. After receiving the vicar's report, Leo issued a directive which concluded by saying that all other questions should be treated in provincial synods and the results reported to him. The pope dealt with the African province as if it had been subject to him for years. And yet Augustine had been dead only a little more than ten years!

To understand fully the change and the magnitude of the position of Leo I one has to appreciate the attitude of the African church toward Rome in the age of Augustine. From 402 to 417 Innocent I was pope; he was by far the most important bishop of Rome before Leo. African synods and Augustine himself turned to Innocent with the request that he condemn Pelagius and his doctrine. They did this in an appropriate manner but without subordinating themselves to the Roman claims of power. Augustine even instructed Innocent in detail on correct theology. Innocent concurred with the African wishes and condemned Pelagius. He pretended that the Africans had sought his decision and had turned to him because they were convinced that nothing was valid without the consent of the bishop of Rome. In reality, however, Innocent was forced to let his course be set by Augustine and the African synods.

When Innocent's successor Zosimus spoke in favor of Pelagius and Caelestius in a rather forceful way, he had to accept a rather sharp reply from Africa. Even after he had begun to extricate himself from his position, a synod which was attended by more than two hundred bishops met in Africa in 418; it reformulated the African point of view and declared that the decision of Innocent was still valid. When the emperor also upheld the Africans, Zosimus had no choice but to confess his defeat by publicly announcing a new decision against Pelagius. After this Augustine made use of a Roman clergyman, a friend of his, to fight against the machinations of the Pelagians in Rome.

Later, in order to restore his position in Africa, Zosimus sent a delegation to assert his rights as chief shepherd. But the delegation returned without having achieved its purpose. When Zosimus' successor, Boniface I, renewed the attempt, a council was convened in 419 which again was attended by more than two hundred African bishops and which frustrated this attempt also. The third attempt, in 426, which Caelestinus I made in the same matter had a disastrous outcome for Rome. Africa not only forbade a legate's ever again being sent to its territory, it questioned generally the right of the Roman bishop to send delegates to direct non-Roman affairs. This position was stated in language which accused Rome only too clearly of presumption and haughtiness. The Africans maintained that their clergy were subject to their own judgment, the lower ranks as well as the bishops. If one of them should feel wrongly condemned, he would be free to turn to the provincial synod or to an ecumenical council. How could the Roman bishop beyond the sea evaluate matters correctly from such a distance! No one could believe that God would confer what was tantamount to infallible judgment upon a single individual, and deny it to a large number of bishops assembled in a provincial synod.

All this must be borne in mind when looking at the decisions of Leo I concerning the election of bishops in Africa, which were made less than twenty years later. It is completely right if one points out that the invasion of the Vandals had basically changed the situation of the church of Africa. The Vandals had not only conquered the province, they also had the greater part of the country ceded to them by the peace treaty of 442. The bishop's see of Carthage was now Arian; Catholicism existed officially only in one part of the country and throughout most of the country it was a persecuted communion. So we can see that the change in the African church was not essentially the achievement of Leo, but it was characteristic of his time.

Already at the time of Innocent I the Germanic tribes had overpowered Rome for the first time (in 410 under Alaric). Leo I went through similar crises during the invasion of the Huns under Attila in 452, and in 455 during the invasion of Gaiseric. The Roman Empire in the West began to totter and soon collapsed completely, and the Germanic tribes extended over its whole area. The old era was passing away. The East went its own way as far as both the church and the state were concerned. Only during Justinian's reign was there a temporary period of restoration. The unity of the world was broken, and it was necessary to find the path which would lead from one age into another.

At this great turn of events stood Leo I, who was later given the surname "the Great" by the church. That which his predecessors had introduced he brought to completion. Innocent had steadily attempted to subject the church of the West to the scepter of the bishop of Rome. What he began was finished under Leo I. The changing of the times contributed decisively to this. Yet Leo I is to be admired for the purposefulness with which he put to use the inheritance he had received.

The first to do so, Leo claimed and bore the title "Vicar of Peter." He was truly a pope after the fashion of the great bishops of Rome in the Middle Ages. Because of the circumstances of the time, his actual power was still limited. Soon after him these limits were tightened by the Germans and by Byzantium. But this lasted only as long as the state had the power to do so. In the measure in which the external pressure decreased, the extension of papal power increased until we see it in its glory during the Middle Ages. But by the middle of the fifth century the papacy as such, personified by Leo the Great, was a finished product.

JUSTINIAN

A New Age Dawns

The Council of Chalcedon was a doctrinal success for the West. Even if the declaration of the supremacy of Constantinople in the East had put a drop of bitterness in the cup of joy, nevertheless, the defeat of 449 at the "Robber Synod" had been balanced. Leo I, through his delegates, had played a role at the council which lived up to the role he claimed as bishop of Rome. The emperor also could be satisfied that the controversies of nearly a century had been concluded. Furthermore, the six hundred bishops assembled at the council, except for a negligible minority, had agreed with the council's doctrinal decision with enthusiastic applause.

Strange to say, just two years earlier many of these very same bishops had just as enthusiastically approved the diametrically opposed doctrinal position. Antiochian theologians and all who were sympathetic to their way of thinking were able to sign the council's confession with good conscience. Even Nestorius could have done so without hesitation. He was still living at the time of Chalcedon and saluted the council from exile and imprisonment, for even the Council of Chalcedon could not give him his freedom. Cyril of Alexandria, who was praised so highly as the example of orthodoxy in the confession of the council, could have signed it only with great effort and considerable reinterpretation.

But the Egyptians of the year 451 could not sign it at all. Despite all urging, the representatives of the Egyptian church refused to subscribe to the Council's decision, declaring that they would rather be beaten to death at Chalcedon for not signing than be beaten to death at home for signing. Thus the Council of Chalcedon did not quench the fire of the controversies; its confession became a torch on which the flame of ecclesiastical and theological discord was lighted anew. Actually the decision of Chalcedon was unacceptable to the whole Egyptian church, with the exception of a part of the upper class in Alexandria itself, and to monasticism, which had been increasingly influenced by Cyril, whose thinking expressed a certain attitude existent in the church since long before Anthanasius. For them Christ was not of two natures but became one nature out of two. Their stress was on the Logos, who indeed put on flesh, but who was God on earth. This Logos had one nature, namely, the divine, although to this divine nature was added the existence in the flesh. For them man's salvation seemed assured if they could see God immediately in Christ and be certain of his absolute divinity. They held that men participated in divinity in the Lord's Supper, which communicated the real substance of God to men and elevated them to God and made them participants in him. Only on the basis of the unambiguous acceptance of this one nature in Christ was a truly pious life and true church possible to them. Any statement which restricted this one nature in any way endangered not only the church but also one's own salvation; it was, therefore, from Satan and had to be resisted to the death.

Thus after Chalcedon the so-called Monophysitic controversies ensued for approximately a century and were characterized at times by an intense bitterness. Soon after Chalcedon the controversies led to a bloody revolt in Egypt which was suppressed only with much difficulty. No sooner was it put down there than Egyptian monks carried it over into Palestine. Chalcedon became a symbol either to rally around or to attack. Bishops were expelled or appointed depending on whether they spoke for or against the decision of the Council. Thus there were times when in the East only a few scattered islands of Chalcedonian orthodoxy dotted the sea of Monophysitism. In addition to this strife, there were other vehement conflicts taking place within the empire, and these, too, resulted in decisions that affected imperial policies toward the church. Also, among the Monophysites themselves there were theological divisions which introduced another complicating factor into the fight against the Chalcedonians and also had an influence on the election of bishops. Many efforts were made to mediate the various controversies, but these efforts only confused the situation. The complexity of the events was increased still further by the fact that national passions were added to the religious ones. All these factors must be taken into account if we want to understand what happened to the Eastern church from approximately 450-550.

The controversies came to a conclusion at the fifth ecumenical council at Constantinople in the year 553. If we were to summarize its results in one sentence, we would have to say that here the attempt was made to relate the Chalcedonian formulas to the thought world of Cyril and thereby to that of the moderate Monophysites. Chalcedon was therefore interpreted according to Cyril, and the unity of the natures was emphasized strongly; all attempts to let the distinctness of the natures be of more than theoretical significance were rejected. In other words, all Antiochian interpretations, which were completely admissible according to the confession of Chalcedon, were rejected.

This decision and the Council which made it were the work of Emperor Justinian. From the time he became sole ruler in 527 he had worked in this direction. Although he favored the Chalcedonian position and his wife Theodora, the Monophysites, Justinian felt that the emphases of the theology of Cyril were much more congruent with the issues than those of Leo I and the Western tradition. Therefore he attempted to counter the latter and to strengthen the former. Naturally one might assert that Justinian's attitude was politically motivated. If he wanted peace and allegiance from the southeast of his empire, he had to assume a friendly attitude toward the Monophysites. However, to go over to them completely was impossible for he also had to take the West into consideration. The Catholic church and the pope could not be alienated; otherwise the goal of the conquest or complete winning over of those areas that were ruled by Arian Germans would be jeopardized.

It is claimed that Justinian took a position which retained the decision of Chalcedon but softened it in the direction of the Monophysite views precisely because of these political considerations. It could also be mentioned that in 531 the plight of the Monophysites was alleviated by Justinian, who permitted their banished leaders to return, and that in 543 the emperor condemned Origen and the leading Antiochian theologians, Theodore of Mopsuestia, Theodoret of Cyrus, and Ibas of Edessa. In addition, Justinian forced the reluctant West to consent to the condemnation of the Antiochians. But this does not tell the full story. For almost at the same time the emperor opposed the Monophysites and even banned Severus, the leader of their more moderate wing, from Constantinople. The decision proclaimed by the Council in 553, which was practically nothing more than the ecclesiastical confirmation of an imperial decision, was completely in accord with the position of Justinian. He wanted to lead to this point of view all who deviated from it, be it to the left (the West, which basically agreed with the Antiochians), or to the right (the Monophysites).

In the West, Justinian succeeded to a large extent with the help of weak and submissive popes. But things went differently in the East. Here it was indeed possible to restrain Monophysitism by force. Still, the East could not be won over inwardly, even if one attempted to meet it halfway. For even in this case a limitation of the true Monophysite conceptions and doctrines remained, and such a limitation was unbearable in the eyes of the intolerant Monophysite groups that were strongly influenced by monasticism. The Monophysites could be only what they were or they would be unfaithful to themselves. But even these failures did not discourage

Justinian. His attitude in the christological question was not determined from the outside, by political considerations, but from the inside, by a well-defined theological and religious attitude.

Let us not forget that Justinian was also a theologian as well as a statesman. In his person as in his whole empire two areas were merged into one. And in this case it was not that the statesman influenced the theologian, but that the theologian influenced the statesman. We need only to read the theological writings which Justinian published under his name (even though he may actually have written very little of them himself), to see this clearly. The statesman had influence here only so far as he forced the theologian in Justinian to make certain concessions or to take certain detours now and then which were forced on him by the political situation. The theologian determined the goal and the overall attitude.

Once more Justinian unified those forces which had influenced the centuries we have reviewed so far. He restored the Roman Empire. When he began his reign, his rule was limited to the East, from Albania down to the Cyrenaica. When he died, he had taken Italy and the areas of the east coast of the Adriatic Sea, Northern Africa, the south of Spain, and the islands of the Mediterranean Sea from the Germans. And this empire was filled by the Roman spirit, ruled according to Roman law and in the Latin language. The rule of the emperor was uncontested; he made all the decisions concerning public, cultural, and religious life. The church embraced all provinces of the empire in a bond of unity, as had paganism of old.

Justinian regarded himself as the executor of the heritage of the past, and he could claim that he fulfilled this task—a gigantic achievement if the circumstances under which it was carried out are considered. In five years he compiled the laws of past centuries into one unified code which remained in effect for over a millennium. And the man who hardly ever went beyond the walls of Constantinople and never performed a warlike act himself was able, through his generals, to bring about the downfall of the kingdoms of the Germans, although at that very moment the danger threatening from the Persians was greater than ever.

Yet Justinian's work was only of short duration, and the splendor of his reign is deceiving. Restoration of the Roman Empire? Yes, but the empire was smaller than at the time of Caesar, and what is more, it did not endure long. The Langobards invaded Italy, and in North Africa as well as in Spain and Egypt the Arabs extinguished the work of Justinian so thoroughly that few traces of the Roman period are still left. And although Justinian wanted to imbue his empire with the Roman spirit, the reality was that despite the official use of the Latin language, these areas had been influenced by other factors.

Justinian had cut through the connections with antiquity and brought about something new without intending to do so. He had made possible the Byzantine Empire that, largely influenced by him, existed for a millennium, even though it was limited to a narrow area between the Germanic powers in the West and the Great Empire of the Persians, and after them the Arabs, in the East.

And the church as the bond of unity of the empire? East and West could not be held together permanently. This was shown even in the concluding stages of the christological controversy in which the development of the so-called Monenergistic and Monotheletic controversies (one or two energies in Christ; human or divine will ruling in him?) led again from Justinian's basically friendly attitude toward Monophysitism to a stance determined by the West. The sixth ecumenical council at Constantinople 680/81 spoke of two natural wills and two energies in the one Christ. That was the counter-effect to the Council of 553 which, under Justinian's influence, steered an Eastern course. It is characteristic that the East looked to the synod of 692, the Trullanum, as a continuation of the sixth ecumenical council and made decisions there which were emphatically rejected by the West. Later a controversy about images would further separate the two sections of the church. Independent separate development of the churches of East and West could not be stopped; nor could the splitting off of the national churches of Egypt, Syria, Persia, and Armenia.

Justinian wanted to do the impossible. Once more the world would have been united into one as in earlier centuries. But this could no longer be achieved permanently, for a new age had dawned. This happened in the epoch of the controversies over the two natures of Christ. They lasted almost three hundred years. When they began, the empire under Theodosius and the church were still united. When they ended, the empire had fallen apart and was on its way to the proliferation of states which characterized the Middle Ages. The foundation had been laid for a divided church: the Catholic in the West and the Orthodox in the East.